HUSBANDS
STEP UP YOUR GAME:

LEAD.
LOVE.
BUILD.
FIGHT.

GARY & JENNIFER RASH

Husbands Step Up Your Game:
LEAD. LOVE. BUILD. FIGHT.
©2018 Gary and Jennifer Rash

Print ISBN: 9781945464270

eBook ISBN: 9781945464287

Published by: Gary and Jennifer Rash

Cover Design – Christine Dupre

Interior Design – Lisa Thomson

CONTENTS

FOREWORD

"Husbands Step Up Your Game: Lead. Love. Build. Fight. is a very challenging men's devotional guide, that will be greatly used by God to empower men to fulfill their purpose as Godly men, husbands, and fathers.

It has been my privilege to personally know Gary and Jennifer Rash for over twenty years. Our relationship has developed as friends, church members, staff members of the church I pastored, and as they served as senior pastors in the international ministerial fellowship that I served as bishop for almost twenty years. Gary and Jennifer are ever growing in their walk with God, each other in their marriage, and in their family life. In character, conduct, and consistency they are committed to living out a Christ-like life that is reflected in their role as authors.

Never in my lifetime has Christian manhood, marriage, and family been in greater need of biblical and practical models for men to fulfill their God-given roles of husbands and fathers. The current crisis is the result of significant negative cultural shifts, from undefined or redefined roles for men, which are unbiblical and unhealthy.

Gary and Jennifer have captured and conveyed clearly, the true biblical picture of a godly, growing man who is fulfilling his roles as a husband by leading, loving, building, and fighting for the marriage and family God has designed for all of us.

Men, read this book and you will be challenged, encouraged, and empowered to become everything God created you to be when He declared: "Let us make man in our image, according to our likeness... male and female He created them. Then God blessed them."

– Dr. Paul Gaehring, former President of Redemption Ministerial Fellowship International, an international network ministry of 1500 ministers, ministries, and para-church ministries.

"As I read through this book, the honor and privilege of writing the foreword began to feel like a responsibility to get the word out on its importance: Lives are at stake. Society is at stake. That's how important I came to know this book to be. The family unit is under attack. The Enemy knows it to be the cornerstone of every society. He also knows that the man is the cornerstone of every family. So, the husband has become the point of attack. This book not only shows the husband how to take his place and keep it, but it equips him to be the Leader, Lover, Builder, and Defender God created him to be.

Gary and Jennifer Rash are well suited to write this book. Countless marriages have been reclaimed, revitalized, and restored as a testament to the grace on their lives in this area. As co-laborers with them and fellow leaders of the God Invasion revival movement, I have firsthand account of their lives and ministry. Their humility not only hides a deep well of Grace for breathing life into marriages but decades of practical experience.

The book *Husbands Step Up Your Game: Lead. Love. Build. Fight.* does what so many books fail to: It ministers to you the practical "How To." It does not scream at you about every place where you have missed it and then leave you hanging. It helps you to get a Vision for Transformation lovingly helping you to build a personal roadmap for your life and family.

I know I have focused in on the men. However, Ladies, I feel this book is a must for you also. I strongly believe that it will give you keen insight and a strong prayer foundation for the men in your lives.

As Bishop to more than 30 churches and 3 schools in 7 countries, I see the trauma and cost in lives daily when the husband refuses to step up and walk in his role. This book will help and is a must-have. Pastors and Leaders, I encourage you to share this book with your men. For all of you Men, I feel this book should be a daily companion with your Bible. While reading, I kept being reminded of things to do, things not to do; and of, things I should be praying. However, I was not left beaten down by where I was missing it, but I was continually being built up and refreshed by the Grace and Love pouring out of the pages and the desire in my heart to be better. Every chapter reminded me of how important my role was as a husband and how it affected every aspect of my life and the lives of those around me. Proverbs 23:23 impresses upon us the importance of God's Truth, Wisdom, Instruction and Understanding and that is what you will find on every page of this book."

– Dr. Byron Corbitt, Pastor of Antioch New Life Christian Center in Simpsonville, South Carolina. Overseer of more than 30 churches and ministries worldwide as well as three schools in seven nations. He serves as Bishop and International Missionary for the World for Christ Commission.

HUSBANDS STEP UP YOUR GAME: LEAD. LOVE. BUILD. FIGHT.

INTRODUCTION

Note from the authors:

Brothers in Christ, it is imperative that we understand how significant our role as men really is. *Husbands, Step Up Your Game: Lead. Love. Build. Fight.* is a call to husbands to step back into their God-ordained role, leading their families, loving their wives just as Christ loved the church, building strong and solid marriages, and recognizing that their marriages are worth fighting for.

Marriage and the family are the bedrock of society. When there is a breakdown in the marriage and the family, we will begin to see the deterioration of society as a whole. Isn't this what we are seeing today? We can look around and see a nation that is in moral decline. We see a culture that calls evil good and good evil. We are now seeing an identity crisis among our young people like we've never seen before. Where did it all begin? It began when men started giving their strength away. As men turned their backs on their responsibilities and stopped functioning in their God-ordained roles, the very fabric of society began to unravel. When men fail to understand the significance of God's mission and their position, there is a breakdown that begins to take place. When men abandon their God-given assignments, the result will be dysfunction.

Over the span of the last twenty years, I have seen the deterioration of the family unit. I worked with teenagers and young men who came out of broken homes, who had no fathers present in their lives and some who did not even know who their fathers were. We have been aware of a fatherless generation struggling among us for quite some time. We have also seen society's image of men change from a very positive light to a very negative light. Television shows began portraying husbands and fathers as weaklings. And then we entered into a gender war that has been feminizing and even emasculating men.

1

Emasculate – to deprive (a man) of his male role or identity. To make a person weaker or less effective. Synonyms: weaken, enfeeble, debilitate, erode, undermine, cripple, remove the sting from, pull the teeth out of.

Today, we have men who believe they are women, and women who believe they are men, and everything in between. The ever-changing culture around us has attempted to define and redefine things for us like biological genders and the institution of marriage. We have been fed the lie that we must tolerate and accept anything and everything. As men with integrity speak up concerning the issues of right and wrong in the world today, their speech is referred to as hate speech. More and more, good men have been losing their courage. They have become silent. They have faded into the background and we see the eroding of society because of it. Men of God, it's time to take our manhood back and take our identity back. We cannot allow the culture around us to define things for us. We certainly cannot allow it to define who we are as men, as husbands, and as fathers. There should be no confusion about our identity. Even if nobody has ever affirmed us in any way, we can still go all the way back to the beginning and find these words in Genesis 1:27:

"So God created man in His own image; in the image of God He created him; male and female He created them." (NKJV)

We have been created in God's own image and it is time for us to become image bearers. God is calling us to the front line. It is time for us to begin functioning in our God-given call as godly husbands and leaders. We have been called, appointed, and anointed for this role. It is God's desire that we have marriages and families that are strong, healthy, and thriving. God has not set us up to fail but to succeed. I urge you to take courage and move ahead with strong determination and purpose. There is an urgency in this hour that we are living in to step up and become the role models to this next generation when it comes to just what a godly husband who loves his wife and family is supposed to look like, before no more role models can be found. We must begin, now, to lay down the blueprint for our children and grandchildren to follow when it comes to just what a Christian marriage and a Christian home are supposed to represent. We don't have time to dabble in a little bit of sin here and there. We don't have time to waste in complacency. We have got to get this thing right. It's just that important. What we do, or do not do will make a lasting impact on the world around us. So, men of God, walk in your God-given role. Fulfill your calling. Let's just go ahead and be what we were made to be.

– *Gary Rash*

> "So since we find ourselves fashioned into all those excellently formed and marvelously functioning parts in Christ's body, let's just go ahead and be what we were made to be." – Romans 12:5-6 (MSG)

Gentlemen, WE NEED YOU TO DO YOUR PART! *Husbands, Step Up Your Game: Lead. Love. Build. Fight.* is a companion book to the 31-day women's devotional book for wives entitled *The Path to Becoming a Proverbs 31 Wife*. Once I completed and released the women's devotional book for wives, I immediately knew that Gary and I would have to get busy creating the men's companion book. I could clearly see that women were going to become very frustrated as they got ahold of the truths within this women's devotional book and began to apply them with all their hearts. I realized that if wives became purposeful about walking in their role to the best of their ability while their husbands made very little effort to recognize and walk in theirs, they would soon feel frustrated, hopeless, and defeated. The Lord confirmed this when I was asked to bring this book into a local church ministry to do a group study with their women. What a wonderful time we had as the Lord began to really speak to wives about the areas in which they needed to change and grow. In fact, women began to testify that the truths within the book had been "life-changing" for them. There was such a sincerity within every single woman to become just what the Lord had created her to be as a wife. These women were filled with a new determination and a great sense of purpose. They longed to have strong, loving, healthy marriages that were thriving. They were more than willing to do their part and they were excited about it, too. Then the question was asked over and over again, "Is there a book for our husbands?" Each woman expressed the desire and the need for good solid teaching to be put in the hands of their husbands as well. This scenario continued to play out as *The Path to Becoming a Proverbs 31 Wife* went around the world. Today, Gary and I are very happy to finally release the much needed and much-requested men's companion book, and what I want to say to you today, gentlemen, is this: If you are going to have a Proverbs 31 treasure of a wife who is more than willing and even enthused about giving you her best, then you had better STEP UP YOUR GAME.

– *Jennifer Rash*

> "I don't know about you, but I'm running hard for the finish line. I'm giving it everything I've got. No sloppy living for me!"
> – 1 Corinthians 9:26 (MSG)

LEAD

"For the husband is the head of the wife, as also Christ is head of the church; and He is the Savior of the body." – Ephesians 5:23 (NKJV)

HUSBANDS STEP UP YOUR GAME: LEAD. LOVE. BUILD. FIGHT.

DAY 1

I AM CALLED TO LEAD

"For the husband is head of the wife, as also Christ is head of the church; and He is the Savior of the body." – Ephesians 5:23 (NKJV)

The Bible uses the word "head" in Ephesians 5:23 when it speaks to the leadership role of a husband. The husband's appointed position and divine purpose are to provide the leadership in his marriage relationship and home. God, Himself, has called us to this position. It is a significant position. Truthfully, we know that we should be operating in this leadership role, but many men do not truly understand just what this role requires, or what exactly it looks like.

Many of us have not seen this biblical leadership role modeled in our own homes growing up. We have not had any real examples before our eyes throughout our lives. Virtually, we have had no one to teach us. No one has given us any tools to work with. We have had little to no training. We have simply done the best we can with the little that we know.

Leadership

Let's begin with what we do know about leadership. When we think of leadership, it is easy to recall many noted leaders of the past. If I were to ask you to name a few leaders, you could probably name at least three. I think of men like William Wallace who was one of the main leaders of the Scottish rights for freedom. Wallace was a remarkable man of great courage. He was said to have almost single-handedly created the determination within his people to stand up and fight back against their oppressors. He was true to his word and he was true to his country. Wallace was appointed Guardian of Scotland.

He paved the way for many victories in Scotland right up until the time he was captured and executed. This was a man who would not compromise and was willing to die for his people's freedom. He is seen by the Scots today as one of their greatest heroes and a martyr for the cause of independence. His life of bravery inspired great literature and even films like *Braveheart*.

Men like Martin Luther King Jr. come to my mind as well. King was an American Baptist minister and activist who led in the African-American Civil Rights Movement. He is best known for his role in the advancement of civil rights using nonviolent civil disobedience based on his Christian beliefs. During his days of boycotts and peaceful demonstrations, King was arrested, his home was bombed, and he was subjected to personal abuse. He was a Christian man of great faith and tenacity. His role in the advancement of racial equality was instrumental in the early 60's. Without a doubt, this man paved the way for African Americans to gain civil rights. His speech, "I Have a Dream" is considered by many to be one of the greatest speeches ever given. King was awarded five honorary degrees, was named Man of the Year by *Time* magazine in 1963 and was the youngest man to ever receive the Nobel Peace Prize when it was awarded to him in 1964. Not only did he become a symbolic leader of African Americans, but Martin Luther King Jr. also became a world figure. And like William Wallace, King gave his very life for his cause when he was assassinated on April 4, 1968.

Ironically, I am also reminded of another leader who was *not* such a great man, Adolf Hitler. Hitler was a leader. He was just a demented, power hungry, antichrist leader. His ability to persuade others to follow him is archived in the annals of history. He systematically and demonically led millions to their death in the gas chambers of Nazi concentration camps. Over 11 million people died due to his leadership ability. You could say that he *succeeded* as a leader. Now that is something to think about, isn't it?

There have been powerful leaders all throughout history who have used their influence for good and even for evil. It is important, then, for us to define this word leadership.

A leader can be defined as "a person who leads someone or something, the one in charge, and a person who convinces other people to follow." A great leader inspires other people and moves them into action.

If you have ever gone to a leadership training event you have learned just what qualities a good leader possesses. A good leader has the ability to communicate effectively and he also knows how to actively listen. A leader encourages and inspires others. He can motivate others and even empower them. His optimism is a source of positive energy and it is contagious among others. A good leader treats people the way he wants to be treated. He is aware of other's needs and he is genuinely concerned for their welfare. An extraordinary leader praises people when things are going well. And when problems arise, he quickly identifies them, seeks solutions, and gets things back on track. He can initiate and implement needed change. When things are going wrong, a good leader will take responsibility for everyone's performance, including his own. He will also work quickly to improve the situation. A leader must make tough decisions. It's part of the position. He has the ability to deal with difficult people and conflict. He has courage. He is committed, and he leads by example. A good leader is humble and patient. He is a good manager of his time. And a good leader earns the respect of the team.

You and I know what it is like to be under someone's leadership. We work under supervisors, managers, crew or team leaders every day. We are very familiar with these things. I have worked for several companies during my lifetime. Some of them were good companies with great leadership. Looking back on those years with those companies, I can honestly say that I enjoyed my time there. On the other hand, I have also worked for a large company whose management was terrible. Anyone else?

I worked under a supervisor once who just did not have a lick of management skills. His production strategy was to threaten the employees and push them to the brink of exhaustion. There was always an overhanging threat that you could and would be replaced. If you didn't like the way you were being treated, too bad. You could leave! Plenty of people were looking for a job just like yours. Can I tell you what the overall work environment and morale was like in that place? Daily, people were blowing their stacks. The way that this supervisor communicated things to the crew did not motivate any of them to work harder. That's for sure. Production stalled. A little praise would have gone a long way. After all, a million things were going right. Instead, like many places of employment, there were meetings where the team was berated for a few inconsistencies, raked over the coals for that one mistake, and never recognized for a job well done. Individuals were never given any credit for anything. And they certainly weren't compensated enough. Raises and bonuses were unheard of. No one was happy. Most people were noticeably angry. Everyone had a bad attitude. Every day teammates would complain one to another, "I hate this job. I'm getting out of this place." One by one, we did.

How many of us can relate to a poor work environment due to poor management? A company or business can rise or fall according to its management and leadership.

Have you ever been a part of a project that you were really excited about, but the person who was put in charge was less than qualified? Maybe this guy lacked the proper training or maybe he just didn't care. Maybe he didn't have a bit of interest or passion for the position, but nevertheless, this was the individual heading up the project. And it stretched your patience to the max to operate under his leadership.

I was under a leader once who was just plain lazy. The project and everyone involved had so much potential, yet no one involved ever reached any of that potential. This kind of leader hinders and holds back those who are under him. And a leader who doesn't do his part will not inspire anyone. It is very unlikely that he will have any success. Have you ever been under this kind of leadership? You wait for the individual to step up and when he doesn't, you begin to lose respect for him. You experience frustration. You might even think to yourself, "I can do a way better job than this guy!" Yet, within the circumstances, he is the head and you are not. You understand position and authority, so you submit to this person's leadership, but you are not happy about it. You yourself may be doing your job as well as you possibly can, but eventually, you grow very dissatisfied. That excitement that you once had fizzles out.

I am talking to a lot of men. We can all relate to one of these situations. We know the frustration and dissatisfaction associated with having to be under a poor manager, supervisor or leader of some kind, whether it is on the job or in any arena.

Now, imagine our wife's and our family's experience when we have given little thought or care to the way we are operating in our role as the head.

In a very real sense, we have a team and we are the captain. We are the manager or leader of our own crew and we have the potential to do one of two things. We can either create a positive environment where things are running smoothly. It's a productive environment, one that everyone enjoys being in. Or, we can create an environment which feels quite miserable to be a part of. Like the workplace that I just described, the team members have mounting frustrations. They are ready to blow. They can't imagine spending the rest of their lives in this environment.

How have you been leading? What kind of living environment have you created through your leadership in your marriage and home? These are hard questions that must be answered. This is an area of our lives we are going to have to take an honest look at if we are ever going to have the kind of marriage that God has purposed for us to have.

Why don't you take a few minutes right now to think about just what kind of qualities you believe make up a great leader? Make a list of your own. You might even want to skim back through the last few pages prayerfully and underline any leadership qualities that you know you need to grow in. Let's ask the Lord right now to develop and strengthen us in these very areas.

PRAYER

Lord, I really do desire to be a good leader in my marriage and home. I understand that this is a role that You have ordained for me and a position that You have appointed to me. Help me in the areas that I have been failing in. Show me how to take responsibility in the areas where I have simply dropped the ball. Teach me how I can be a better leader, especially in the areas that my wife needs me to be the most. From this day forward, I will be intentional and purposeful in the way that I lead. Lord, let me lead in a way that creates a positive environment. Let me lead in a way that brings about inspiration rather than frustration. Help me to lead in a way that causes our marriage and the life we are building together to thrive. Develop me into the kind of leader that my wife and family can trust and respect, and the kind of leader that they are more than willing to follow. Help me to truly become the strong leader that You have created me to be.

DAY 2

I AM A MAN WITH A VISION

"For the husband is the head of the wife, as also Christ is head of the church; and He is the Savior of the body." – Ephesians 5:23 (NKJV)

In Ephesians 5:23, we see that God has appointed men to a position of leadership in their marriages and homes. We have only begun to take a look at leadership in a general way, but we are already getting a strong impression that our own leadership has the potential to either make or break a thing. Our marriages and our households can either flourish or fail depending on the leadership that you and I exhibit. We can see the importance of good leadership everywhere we look.

Merriam-Webster defines a leader as a person who leads: such as a guide, conductor, or director. These are some interesting examples. When I think of a guide, I immediately think of a tour guide. A tour guide becomes an expert concerning the place where you happen to be traveling. Most likely it's somewhere you've never been before. Typically, this type of guide would be leading you on an adventure of a lifetime. He would stop and point out special points of interest and make sure you enjoyed the scenery. He would make sure you didn't miss the highlights. This guide may even need to help you navigate through rough terrain, difficult areas, or lead you safely through places of danger. Generally, men tend to thrive on risk and danger and are hard-wired for adventure. Women, on the other hand, desire to be taken on an adventure. With that in mind, I challenge you today, gentlemen. Begin leading in a way that causes your marriage to become an adventure of a lifetime. Guide her.

The next example given within Merriam-Webster's definition is that of a conductor. Personally, that presents a very strong image for me. I will never forget what the Lord showed me several years ago when my wife and I had an opportunity to go to the symphony in Charleston, SC. The funny thing is that I was not particularly enthusiastic about going. A neighbor, however, wanted to bless us with the tickets. I really wasn't sure that I would enjoy this kind of thing or not. My wife, on the other hand, saw this as a wonderful opportunity to get dressed up and go out for a beautiful evening together. She was excited, and that was all that was important to me. When we arrived at the auditorium, we quickly found our seats, which were excellent seats, by the way. Jennifer, as usual, looked stunning and I enjoyed her beauty as I waited for the symphony to begin. The crowd was buzzing, and many people were saying how glad they were to be there. I wasn't sure why I was there, honestly. It wasn't something that I would have chosen to do. As I sat there in my seat, I said, "Lord, I don't know what You want to show me or tell me tonight, but here I am."

It wasn't long until I saw a door at the back of the stage open and out came a few people with horns in their hands. Then almost like clockwork, more people entered in through the other doors each one carrying an instrument in their hands. Violinists, cymbalists, percussionists, and wind instrumentalists all took their places on the stage, each one knowing exactly where to stand or sit. Then it seemed all chaos broke out. The violinists began to play their violins in what seemed like a screeching sound of disorder. Next, the cellist started playing their cellos in a different tune that caused the sound to get even worse. The horns blew. The drums beat. The cymbals clanged, but none of it sounded anything like a melody. Imagine, if you will, one hundred people picking up an instrument that they could play well, but each one played their own song. Each one seemed to be doing their own thing. It didn't sound like music to me. It didn't fit together because no one was leading them.

Then it happened. Suddenly, the lights dimmed and out of the center rear stage door walked a distinguished looking man dressed in a dark tuxedo. As if on cue, the instruments became silent. The conductor gently bowed toward the audience and then turned to face the orchestra. He lifted his baton. Everyone on stage came to attention. Then with one swift movement of the baton, something happened. Beautiful, melodic, joy poured forth from the orchestra. It was the most beautiful music I had ever heard. Every note was perfect. Every beat was on rhythm. Every violin was playing in perfect harmony and every wind instrument flowed in mesmerizing unison. It was sweet music to my ears. I was more than impressed! Wolfgang Amadeus Mozart would have been proud.

A conductor is a leader of an orchestra. All the musicians look to him to know when to begin and end the playing of their instruments. Even a leader of a band sets the tempo for the music. Every marriage needs a conductor. That conductor is you. That conductor is me. Our hearts should be beating as one with our spouse. We should be in harmony with one another and God. Our sound should be synchronized. We should be making beautiful music together as husband and wife. As the leaders, you and I are the ones who set the tempo. Are your marriage and home sounding like beautiful, melodic joy, screeching chaos, or somewhere in between? Pick up that baton, fellas. She's waiting on you.

And finally, our last example set forth within our definition today is that of a director. As a movie buff, I can't help but think in terms of film directors. As we know, a film director creates an overall vision for the film itself. He organizes the film crew in a way to achieve the vision of the film. The director ensures that all individuals involved in the film production are all working towards the same vision. He works with the person in charge of each aspect of the film, like writers, set people, those over the lighting, scenery and such, making sure all of the elements are coming together. He guides the technical crew and he makes sure that the actors truly understand the characters that they are portraying. He is an overseer.

The position of a film director is highly stressful and demanding, yet the director has the ability to maintain a singular focus even in the stressful, fast-paced environment of the film set. He is involved in every stage of the film production. In fact, the director spends more time on the project than anyone else. He is in charge of making sure every component of a movie runs smoothly. The director also sees to it that every actor is doing their best work. He must have excellent communication skills. He communicates and directs. He is involved and invested.

How involved and invested are you as the leader of your marriage and home? A man ought to have a vision for his marriage and life together with his spouse. What is your overall vision? Do you have one? If not, ask the Lord to give you a vision.

"Write the vision and make it plain on tablets, that he may run who reads it. For the vision is yet for an appointed time, but at the end it will speak, and it will not lie. Though it tarries, wait for it: because it will surely come. It will not tarry."
– Habakkuk 2:2-3 (NKJV)

Get a God-vision and do whatever you must do to keep your focus.

The Message Bible puts Habakkuk 2:2-3 like this: "**Write it out in big block letters so that it can be read on the run.** This vision-message is a witness pointing to what's coming. It aches for the coming—it can hardly wait! And doesn't lie. If it seems slow in coming, wait. It's on its way. It will come right on time." (emphasis is the author's)

"On the run." That about sums up the pace we feel like we are keeping as we carry out all our daily responsibilities, but what are we running for? And what are we running towards? A man without a vision wanders aimlessly. As the leader and head of your marriage and household, you need a vision. You can't just figure this thing out as you go along. Your wife is counting on you.

Proverbs 29:18 tells us that where there is no vision, people perish. The Message puts it like this; "If people can't see what God is doing, they stumble all over themselves; but when they attend to what he reveals, they are most blessed."

1. Have a vision for your life together.

2. Communicate and share that vision with your spouse. Do it in a way that will cause her to enthusiastically join you in that vision. Pray together about God's plan.

3. Lead in a way that causes the two of you to achieve the vision.

4. Be the kind of man who can manage life's pressures and demands without losing focus of the vision.

What is your vision?

PRAYER

Lord, give me a vision for my marriage and my family. Give me the ability to see what it is that You want for us, Lord. I don't want just any vision. I want a God-vision. Help me to plainly see Your plan and purpose for our life together. Allow that vision to be big enough in my heart that I will always keep it before me and I will never lose sight of it. Help me to become invested and involved in every part of this vision, this purpose, and this plan. And help me to be able to communicate this God-vision in a way that my wife will be more than enthused to partner with me in it. Speak the same things into her heart that you are speaking to mine. Help me to direct the affairs of my marriage and family. Grow me into a strong guide, conductor, and director of our life together. Help me to develop into a leader, a good leader. Shape me and make me into a man with a vision.

DAY 3

I AM A MAN OF INTEGRITY

"For the husband is the head of the wife, as also Christ is head of the church; and He is the Savior of the body." – Ephesians 5:23 (NKJV)

A husband is the head of his marriage and his home. He has a responsibility before God to be the leader. His role is significant. His leadership is critical. We have looked at some pretty important characteristics of a good leader in general, but today we are going straight to the Word of God. One of the keys to becoming a great leader is found in Proverbs 20:7.

> "The righteous man walks in his integrity; His children are blessed after him."

A great leader will always be a person of integrity. What is integrity? Integrity is the quality of being honest and having strong moral and ethical principles and adhering to them. In Proverbs 20:7, this word "integrity" is the word "tom" in the original Hebrew language and it translates as "completeness; moral innocence, uprightness, and to be clean."

Integrity literally speaks of a man who is walking in moral innocence, faithfulness to God and in righteousness through Christ. This is what shapes a man into the right kind of leader.

So important is this characteristic of integrity, it is outlined as a qualification for anyone desiring to be a leader or overseer in the church. Look with me at 1 Timothy 3:1-10.

"This is a faithful saying: If a man desires the position of a bishop, he desires a good work. A bishop then must be blameless, the husband of one wife, temperate, sober-minded, of good behavior, hospitable, able to teach; not given to wine, not violent, not greedy for money, but gentle, not quarrelsome, not covetous; one **who rules his own house well**, having his children in submission with all reverence (for if a man does not know how to rule his own house, how will he take care of the church of God?); not a novice, lest being puffed up with pride he fall into the same condemnation as the devil. Moreover, he must have a good testimony among those who are outside, lest he fall into reproach and the snare of the devil. Likewise, deacons must be reverent, not double-tongued, not given to much wine, not greedy for money, holding the mystery of the faith with a pure conscience. But let these also first be tested; then let them serve as deacons, being found blameless." (NKJV)

This passage is addressing the qualifications of a bishop and deacon, specifically, but I want you to take note of the importance of *ruling one's own house well*. I like the way the Message Bible puts it: "Servants in the church are to be committed to their spouses, attentive to their own children, and diligent in looking after their own affairs."

You see, all ministry of any kind flows out of the home. A man who desires to be a leader in any other arena and especially in the house of God will first be a good leader of his own home. And being a good leader of your own home begins with integrity.

When a man desires to do a good work, especially in the church, there are certain character traits that are deemed necessary in order to fill the position properly. A position of great importance cannot be given to just anyone. Make no mistake about it. The position of a husband is a position of great importance and responsibility. It is possible that you have never considered how vital your role as a husband really is, not just in your own home but even in the community around you. Not only does it carry over into the house of God, but it overflows into the community and it impacts society as a whole. Therefore, this role and this responsibility must become one of your top priorities, even *before* serving in the church. If you cannot serve well in your own home, how will you serve others well in the house of God? Your service will be a natural byproduct overflowing from the love and order in your home. All will be blessed by your leadership. Having things in proper order and alignment sets you up to be blessed and to be a blessing. Even the children of a man who walks in integrity will be blessed.

How are we doing when it comes to having these priorities set in order? Have we been diligently looking after the affairs of our own homes? Are we ruling our homes well?

Let's take a look at this word "rule" in 1 Timothy 3:5. It is the Greek word *proistēmi* and it means to stand before, to preside, to maintain and to oversee. Thayer's Greek Definitions breaks it down like this: To rule is to be over, to superintend, preside over, to be a protector or guardian, to give aid and to care for and give attention to.

Looking closer at this word "rule" helps us to gain some understanding of just how the Lord would have us to walk in our role as the leader of our marriages and homes. Let's ask ourselves some questions in order to evaluate just where our strengths and weaknesses have been.

Have I been ruling my home well?

Have I been committed to my spouse?

Have I been attentive to my children?

When it comes to integrity, am I clean, upright, and do I walk in moral innocence?

Am I an honest man?

Do I have strong moral and ethical principles, and do I adhere to them?

Men, we may not be overseers or leaders over *many* things. We may not be the CEO of a company. We may not be in charge of the operation of an organization. We may not run a crew or supervise a team of workers, and our title may not be the project manager. We may not even be a bishop, a pastor or a deacon. However, we have been appointed as the head of our marriages and our homes. Our wives and our children are under our leadership.

Can your spouse trust you with this very important role?

If we are going to lead with integrity, then we must become men of integrity. Men of integrity keep first things first.

In marriage, there are many firsts, for example; the first home, the first Christmas, and the first child. God's Word tells us about another first in Matthew 6:33.

> "But seek first the kingdom of God and His righteousness, and all these things shall be added to you." – Matthew 6:33 (NKJV)

Listen, there are a lot of things that compete for a husband's time, energy, and focus. One thing, in particular, is our responsibility to bring home the bacon. The majority of our time is spent at our jobs as we focus on providing for the needs of our family. This is part of our role. It is an important part too. Many men in generations before ours prided themselves on being good providers. Some were rarely present in the home because they spent long hours making sure that they had a roof over their family's head and food on the table. They felt that as long as they were good providers, they were good husbands and good fathers. They didn't participate much in the raising of their children. Their responsibility in the home seemed to begin and end with that of providing. My generation and your generation have done a better job at being present and participating in the building of a family. We do, however, place our work first sometimes and it is understandable. We work hard to provide because we need to. Many men struggle to make a living. There is stress and striving that takes place. The struggle is real. We must have provisions, but we must also have a healthy balance and focus.

It is said of some men that they are married to their jobs. If we find ourselves in this place, we have some praying to do. Long work hours leave us depleted and without much left to offer once we arrive home and walk through the door. And like some of our fathers, grandfathers, and great grandfathers, we have forgotten that there is anything more required of us. We forget that our wives have other needs besides provisions. And this is why our main pursuit cannot be finances and worldly goods. Jesus had something to say about the *anxieties* of seeking all of the provisions that we need.

> "Therefore do not worry, saying, 'What shall we eat?' or 'What shall we drink?' or 'What shall we wear?' For after all these things the Gentiles seek. For your heavenly Father knows that you need all these things. But seek first the kingdom of God and His righteousness, and all these things shall be added to you. Therefore do not worry about tomorrow, for tomorrow will worry about its own things. Sufficient for the day is its own trouble." – Matthew 6:31-34 (NKJV)

Our main pursuit cannot be wealth, riches, or material things. And we are not to place ourselves in situations where our minds are consumed with provisions. We must set our hearts on the kingdom of God and trust Him to add all these other things we have need of to our lives as we are faithful to do our part.

Seek first the kingdom of God and His righteousness.

The word "seek" in Matthew 6:33 is the word *zēteō* and it translates as "to desire, endeavor, crave, go after and aim for."

What has been your primary endeavor? What have you been running after and aiming for? When it comes to your marriage, what have you made your first priority?

We must seek the kingdom of God and His righteousness before we seek anything else. His kingdom can be defined as the rule and reign of God over all things. His kingdom also includes His precepts, principles, and workings. His ways are better, higher, and greater than our own ways. We will do well to remember that.

We are to seek first His kingdom and His righteousness. His righteousness can be defined as *integrity*. It is virtue, purity of life, the correctness of thinking, feeling, and acting like Christ.

Integrity.

The Sermon Bible Commentary says this concerning this seeking: "The Lord exhorts us to seek the kingdom of God and His righteousness. This is the pith and the kernel of the whole matter. What He means is, that they are not to set their hearts on the possessions of this world—it's riches and honours, and pampering indulgences and vain displays; neither are they to vex their hearts with cares concerning these, as the Gentiles do, sinking thereby into like degradation with them, but they are to make it there foremost object to obtain spiritual treasures—meekness, temperance, patience, faith, love, and all things just and true and honest and pure and lovely, which are the true riches and real honours of man, the only dignities acknowledged in the kingdom of God. Now the way to obtain these is through faith in God and His Christ. Their great effort, therefore, should be to believe that God reigns, and to trust Him with a most loyal and unswerving devotion."

The main pursuit must be a life that pleases Him. When we are striving to please the Lord, we will find that pleasing our wife comes naturally.

PRAYER

Lord, I pray that I would always be a man of integrity. My desire is to walk blamelessly before you. Help me to keep first things first. Set the priorities of my heart and life in order, Father. Help me to establish order and balance in all that I am doing. Guide me as I seek to meet every one of my daily responsibilities. Meet me right where I'm at as I strive to be a good provider. Make me a good manager and a good steward of my time and energy. Help me to be a man that is committed to my spouse and attentive to my children. Let me be a man who does well when it comes to looking after the affairs of my own marriage and family. Cause me to grow daily in all of these things as I place my trust in You. Today, I understand that the impact my leadership has in my home will actually spill over into my place of employment, my place of worship, the community around me, and even society as a whole. Lord, mold me and shape me into the right kind of leader.

HUSBANDS STEP UP YOUR GAME: LEAD. LOVE. BUILD. FIGHT.

DAY 4

I AM A SERVANT LEADER

"For the husband is the head of the wife, as also Christ is head of the church; and He is the Savior of the body." – Ephesians 5:23 (NKJV)

Husbands, we have been appointed as the head or leader of our marriages and homes and we are to lead well. The mark of a good leader is integrity. 1 Timothy 3:1-10 seems to imply that this overseeing in one's own home must be the first priority before one is fit to oversee and serve elsewhere, and specifically in the church. Paul was addressing the role of bishops and deacons in 1 Timothy chapter three. They are called to be servants in the house of the Lord. In much of the same way, husbands are called to be servant leaders in their own homes. Paul stresses the importance of serving well in our own homes above all other serving. If we cannot serve the woman who we know most intimately, our wife, what makes us think we can serve others effectively?

Serve. Yes, you read that right. Don't get the wrong impression of words like *head* and *rule*. Don't get the wrong idea about your position as the leader of your marriage and home. Galatians 3:28 makes it clear when it says, "There is neither Jew nor Greek, there is neither slave nor free, there is neither male nor female; for you are all one in Christ Jesus." The Bible affirms equality among men and women. God has simply assigned specific roles to each of them. Your role as the head or leader doesn't place you in a dominating position. Leaders serve. Jesus modeled something of this servant leadership as He washed His disciple's feet. Jesus humbled Himself and took on the task of a servant to demonstrate something of great significance to us.

Servanthood

> And He said to them, "The kings of the Gentiles exercise
> lordship over them, and those who exercise authority over
> them are called 'benefactors.' But not so among you; on the
> contrary, he who is greatest among you, let him be as the
> younger, and he who governs as he who serves."
> – Luke 22:25-26 (NKJV)

Jesus was about to change some mindsets as he spoke these words
to His disciples. These men only understood what they had seen and
experienced. They had been under leaders who led with an iron
hand. And just before Jesus spoke these words, an argument between
the disciples had taken place concerning who was going to be the
greatest in the kingdom of God. They believed the Messiah would
set up a kingdom with offices and rankings within the government
of that kingdom. Had these disciples become ambitious for power
and prominence?

Jesus was concerned about their hearts and He began teaching the
disciples kingdom principles. These principles that He taught and
modeled can be described as servant-leadership. A servant leader is
not preoccupied with personal visibility, recognition, or popularity
but instead desires to place the attention upon the one he is serving.

Understand that as Jesus taught and demonstrated these principles,
He was in no way negating authority. He was, however, clarifying
the kind of character and heart attitude in which one is to exercise
authority. There is a right way and a wrong way to walk in a position
of authority. A servant leader always puts those he is serving first.

What a concept. We live in a culture today where everyone around
us seems to be self-absorbed and self-centered. I see a generation of
people who demand their ways, fight for their rights and insist on
being recognized. And if you dare to disagree with their views you
will have many very negative and false labels placed upon you. Many
are prideful. Narcissism reigns. We had better be very careful not to
raise up our children to believe that the entire world revolves around

them. It doesn't. The battle is real today. And I wonder how many of us grown men have had some wrong programming. We need to check ourselves. Someone who is proud and self-centered may become very domineering over those assigned to their care. Someone who is proud and self-centered really has little capacity for love and humility. Jesus was teaching that we should humble ourselves, not lording our authority over those entrusted to us. We are to be examples to those we lead.

> "Now before the Feast of the Passover, when Jesus knew that His hour had come that He should depart from this world to the Father, having loved His own who were in the world, He loved them to the end. And supper being ended, the devil having already put it into the heart of Judas Iscariot, Simon's son, to betray Him, Jesus, knowing that the Father had given all things into His hands, and that He had come from God and was going to God, rose from supper and laid aside His garments, took a towel and girded Himself. After that, He poured water into a basin and began to wash the disciples' feet, and to wipe them with the towel with which He was girded."

> "So when He had washed their feet, taken His garments, and sat down again, He said to them, "Do you know what I have done to you? You call Me Teacher and Lord, and you say well, for so I am. If I then, *your* Lord and Teacher, have washed your feet, you also ought to wash one another's feet. For I have given you an example, that you should do as I have done to you. Most assuredly, I say to you, a servant is not greater than his master; nor is he who is sent greater than he who sent him. If you know these things, blessed are you if you do them."
> – John 13:1-5, 12-16 (NKJV)

Jesus was about to go to the cross and die for all the world and yet He was still concerned about the needs of His disciples. He kept demonstrating His love for them even in His last hours. Their teacher and their Lord lowered Himself to do the job of a servant.

When guests came into a home, it was the task of the lowest servant to wash their feet. That evening, after listening to His disciples bicker over who was going to be the greatest, Jesus took on the task of the lowest slave. It was the task of washing feet. Jesus poured the water into the basin, removed His robe, belt, and tunic, leaving Himself clothed like a slave, and got down on the ground. He washed His disciples' dirty feet, one by one. It must have completely shocked every one of them.

Jesus, the Son of the Most-High God, King of Kings and Lord of Lords, humbled Himself to meet His disciple's needs and He asks us to do the same. It's the kind of leadership that does not rule and govern by lording its authority over someone. One who rules his house well does not do it in a demanding or arrogant way. A good leader is not full of himself nor is he self-centered. Instead, he is a humble servant seeking the best interest of those who have been entrusted to him. And he is faithful to lead according to the example that Jesus Himself has modeled for us.

> "For who is greater, he who sits at the table, or he who serves? Is it not he who sits at the table? Yet I am among you as the One who serves." – Luke 22:27 (NKJV)

I remember the very moment these truths penetrated my heart and thinking. My wife is always serving me and everyone in our household. She puts herself last. It comes naturally to her. She is always thinking of me and doing things for me. Always. I decided on this particular day that I was going to out serve her. And I have become determined to do just that. I challenge you this week to ask your wife this question, "How can I serve you?"

We may very well have a culture around us where many men are self-centered, self-serving, and full of themselves. Let's break that mold.

> "Most men will proclaim every one of his own goodness: but a faithful man who can find? A just man walketh in integrity: his children are blessed after him." – Proverbs 20:6-7 (KJV)

Here it is straight from the book of Proverbs. Most men think pretty highly of themselves and toot their own horns. A faithful man, on the other hand, is hard to find. Let us become faithful in leading with humble hearts.

PRAYER

Lord, I humble myself before you today. Forgive me for any time that I have been demanding and even arrogant. Form in me the right character and heart attitude necessary for leading well. I value my wife and I am thankful that You have entrusted her care to me. Allow me to demonstrate my love for her as I seek her best interest rather than my own. Speak to me about how I can be that servant leader in my own household among those I love the most. Show me how I can follow Your example and in what ways I can serve my wife.

HUSBANDS STEP UP YOUR GAME: LEAD. LOVE. BUILD. FIGHT.

DAY 5

I LEAD WITH WISDOM AND KNOWLEDGE

"For the husband is the head of the wife, as also Christ is head of the church; and He is the Savior of the body." – Ephesians 5:23 (NKJV)

God has appointed you and me as the head of our marriages and homes. As we continue to look at just what it means to be the head, we discover that this position carries responsibility and accountability. Understanding these things humbles us. We don't take this responsibility lightly.

This word "head" is a metaphor taken from the head of the natural body. The strength of the body is the head. The head is the seat of reason, wisdom, and knowledge. If we are going to lead our household, we have got to have wisdom and knowledge to do it.

> Proverbs 24:3 says, "Through wisdom a house is built, and by understanding it is established." (NKJV)

Where do wisdom and knowledge come from? How do I get this wisdom and knowledge?

The Bible tells us that "The fear of the LORD is the beginning of wisdom, and the knowledge of the Holy One is understanding." – Proverbs 9:10 (NKJV)

Psalms 111:10 would add, "The fear of the LORD is the beginning of wisdom; A good understanding have all those who do His commandments; His praise endures forever." (NKJV)

Do you know Him? Are you a man who seeks the Lord? Are you a man of faith? Do you follow His commandments? This leading that we are doing as husbands is anchored in the sure foundation of Jesus Christ. What we are really asking and expecting from our wives is this: "Follow me as I follow the Lord."

Proverbs 2:6 says, "For the Lord gives wisdom; from his mouth come knowledge and understanding." And Job 12:13 says, "To God belong wisdom and power; counsel and understanding are His." (NIV)

Do you know His Word? Do you listen to His voice? Wisdom and knowledge come from the Lord. He gives His wisdom and knowledge to us. The truth is that we need His wisdom and His knowledge more than ever before.

The Word of God tells us that His wisdom and understanding are better than anything else we can acquire. Honor, success, peace, and long life are many of the blessings that flow out of the wisdom and knowledge that come from God. And believe it or not, this wisdom and knowledge are acquired through a humble heart.

> "When pride comes, then comes disgrace, but with humility comes wisdom." – Proverbs 11:2 (NIV)

> "Blessed is the one who finds wisdom, and the one who gets understanding, for the gain from her is better than gain from silver and her profit better than gold. She is more precious than jewels, and nothing you desire can compare with her. Long life is in her right hand; in her left hand are riches and honor. Her ways are ways of pleasantness, and all her paths are peace." – Proverbs 3:13-18 (ESV)

As we lead, we ask the Lord for His wisdom, knowledge, and direction in all that we do. We can't let our human nature get the best of us. We cannot be stubborn or prideful and think that we don't need God.

What is it that men are known for doing when they are driving, and they become unsure of the way to go? How quickly will they admit that they are lost? How long will they wait until they stop and ask someone for directions? Why do we pretend that we know it all?

Pride.

The phrase, "I got this" seems to be the modern mantra of manhood and the inability to fix it all, indicates a weakness in your manhood — according to the world's view.

When I was younger there was a phrase that became popular. It was the phrase "You are the man!" When one of the guys did something great, we would encourage him by telling him, "You are the man!" We love to take full credit for anything that we do right, right? But what about when we fail miserably? And what about when we don't have a clue?

Being "the man" was one thing when we were young and immature. As men become older and more mature, the definition of being a man, changes. Especially, when that man gets married and starts a lifetime of love and commitment to a woman. If we really want to get this manhood thing right, we have got to humble ourselves.

We have got to come to a place and time when we admit that we really don't have all the answers. And we aren't always right about everything. We don't always get it right and we can't fix everything even if we want to. We need the Lord. We need His wisdom. We need Him to show us the right way. We need His guidance and His direction. And we can't guide and direct anyone else well without it.

What have you been depending on? Who is your source? Are you self-sufficient?

The psalmist proclaimed, "My power and my strength come from the LORD, and he has saved me." – Psalm 118:14 (CEV)

David who killed a lion and a bear, slew the giant Goliath, killed 10,000 Philistines, and became a king, always recognized where his strength, power, and authority came from. The Lord referred to

David as a man after His own heart. It's time that you and I become confident men who are after the heart of God.

We aren't big and bad all by ourselves. Our real power and strength come from the Lord. He is our source and there is no other. A strong, confident man filled with power is one who places his life and his trust in God. He is a man of faith. He is led by the wisdom and knowledge of God. In turn, he is able to lead his family well.

As the head of our marriage, we should lead by example in our devotion to the Lord. And we should be able to teach our wives the Word of God. The problem is that many of our wives know the Word way better than we do. Why is that? God is calling us to be the spiritual leaders in our homes.

Can our wives learn something from us when it comes to the things of God?

Are you where you need to be in your relationship with God? Do you study His Word and pray? As the spiritual leader of your home, read the Word of God with your wife. Discuss it with her.

Pray together. You initiate that. And take your family to church to worship together in the house of God. Don't think it makes a difference whether or not you do? Think again.

Take a look at these statistics:

> The typical U.S. Congregation draws an adult crowd that's 61% female, 39% male. This gender gap shows up in all age categories.

> On any given Sunday, there are 13 million more adult women than men in America's churches.

> This Sunday almost 25 percent of married, churchgoing women will worship without their husbands.

> Midweek activities often draw 70 to 80 percent female participants.

The majority of church employees are women (except for ordained clergy, who are overwhelmingly male).

More than 90 percent of American men believe in God, and five out of six call themselves Christians, but only one out of six attend church on a given Sunday. The average man accepts the reality of Jesus Christ but fails to see any value in going to church.

Churches overseas report gender gaps of up to 9 women for every adult man in attendance.

Fewer than 10% of U.S. churches are able to establish or maintain a vibrant men's ministry.

What does this tell us about how well Christian men are leading their homes spiritually? Is it really that important? And isn't it just as good if the wife leads the home spiritually? What difference does it really make? Here are some more statistics that may cause your heart to either sink or soar:

1. When a mother comes to Christ, her family will join her at church only 17% of the time; but when a father comes to Christ, his family joins him 93% of the time.

2. If both father and mother attend regularly, 33 percent of their children will end up as regular churchgoers, and 41 percent will end up attending irregularly. Only a quarter of their children will end up not practicing at all.

3. If the father is irregular and mother regular, only 3 percent of the children will subsequently become regulars themselves, while a further 59 percent will become irregulars. Thirty-eight percent will be lost.

4. If the father is non-practicing and mother regular, only 2 percent of children will become regular worshippers, and 37 percent will attend irregularly. Over 60 percent of their children will be lost completely to the church!

What happens if the father is regular but the mother is irregular or non-practicing? Amazingly, the percentage of children becoming regular goes up from 33 percent to 38 percent with the irregular mother and up to 44 percent with the non-practicing. This suggests that loyalty to the father's commitment grows in response to the mother's laxity or indifference to religion.

According to these studies, if a father does not go to church, no matter how faithful his wife's devotion to Christ is, only one child in 50 will become a regular worshipper. If a father does go regularly, regardless of the practice of the mother, between two-thirds and three-quarters of their children will become churchgoers.

Do these studies confirm that the husband's role as the head is significant? Does his role as the spiritual leader in his marriage and home make a difference? Oh, yeah. If the father takes his faith in God seriously, then the message to his children is that God should be taken seriously. A man has influence in his home. Our leadership makes an impact. We have got to lead by example in our walk with the Lord. It makes a difference in our marriages. It makes a difference in our homes. We will pass down a godly inheritance to our children, and our children's children.

If you have dropped the ball in the past, begin again. Don't feel guilty about it. Don't condemn yourself. There is no need to feel a great sense of failure in what you have not done. Instead, step up to the plate. Become a disciplined leader now.

There is an old saying, "Work like it depends on you. Pray like it depends on God." In other words, give everything that you do your best but understand that everything really does depend on God. Love the Lord your God with all your heart and with all your soul and with all your strength and with all your mind. And remember: "If any of you lacks wisdom, you should ask God, who gives generously to all without finding fault, and it will be given to you." – James 1:5 (NIV)

Lead with the kind of wisdom, knowledge, and understanding that only comes from God. Be the man. Be God's man.

PRAYER

Lord, You are my source. I need Your wisdom, knowledge, and understanding. I need Your direction every day of my life. Help me to become more disciplined than ever before when it comes to my relationship with You, studying Your Word and seeking Your face. I want to be a man after Your own heart, Lord. I want to draw nearer and hear clearer. Lead me, Lord, as I lead my wife. Allow me to become the model to my wife and family when it comes to my devotion to You and my worship before You. I understand the kind of influence that I have and the impact that I make as I walk in my God-given, God-ordained role. I will not take that responsibility lightly. Help me establish and pass down a godly heritage to my children, and my children's children for Your Name's sake, Lord. Fill me with Your strength and Your power as I lead.

"But I want you to know that the head of every man is Christ, the head of woman is man, and the head of Christ is God"
– 1 Corinthians 11:3 (NKJV)

DAY 6

I LEAD WITH A SHEPHERD'S HEART

"For the husband is the head of the wife, as also Christ is head of the church; and He is the Savior of the body." – Ephesians 5:23 (NKJV)

As the leader of our marriages and homes, we too must be led. Jesus is the Good Shepherd who will lead and guide us. He gives us the wisdom and knowledge to lead our marriages and homes well. This is part of our God-ordained role and it includes leading spiritually.

The Expositor's Bible Commentary actually speaks of the perils of neglecting these responsibilities and passing the buck to someone else. It is important that we do not hand over our "priesthood to another man."

> "Christian husbands should take more account of their office than they do; they should not be strangers to the spiritual trials and experiences of the heart so near to them. It might lead them to walk more worthily and to seek higher religious attainments, if they considered that the shepherding of at least one soul devolves upon themselves, that they are unworthy of the name of husband without such care for the welfare of the soul linked to their own as Christ bears toward "His bride the Church." – *The Expositor's Bible Commentary*

The shepherd is one of the best-known metaphors for leadership in the Bible. It is mentioned over 115 times. In the book of Ezekiel, warnings are issued about those leaders referred to as shepherds who have not led or cared for God's people well. Is there a picture anywhere in the Bible of what shepherding well looks like? Absolutely.

Jesus refers to Himself as the Good Shepherd. Psalm 23 describes the way that He shepherds His people. Not only do these well-known scriptures bring us great assurance of His own care for us, but they show us how we, too, must care for those entrusted to our leadership.

In Jesus' day, shepherding was still a vital occupation. When Jesus spoke using terms like shepherds and sheep, the people of His day would have clearly understood the deep spiritual truths expressed and taken them to heart. Today, most men know little to nothing about the occupation of shepherding.

What is the primary role of a shepherd? A shepherd feeds, protects, cares for, and leads his sheep. One of the most important tasks of a shepherd is to feed and water the sheep. The shepherd guides his flock to good pastures and makes sure they have pure water as well. Sometimes a shepherd will actually prepare the pasture for the sheep to graze right where they are at. He may remove stones and thorn bushes. He irrigates the field and builds a hedge. This is hard work. It's a sacrifice of time and energy but he is willing to do whatever is necessary. He is determined that the sheep get the best food and nutrients. In some situations, the shepherd will feed the sheep himself. If there is not pure water available for the sheep, the shepherd draws it from deep wells to water the sheep. Good shepherds know the region and when one pasture is barren, he knows where to find another. With the changing of each season, the shepherd may need to do some planning in order to keep the sheep fed. Water is critical for the sheep to survive. The shepherd knows where the water supplies are. Many times, the sheep are brought to a stream or a river to drink the refreshing water. Sheep, however, do not like troubled waters and often will not drink if the waters are agitated. Sheep can drown in swift flowing waters. Their wool is like a sponge. It absorbs the water and they are weighted down to the extent that they cannot swim. This spells danger and even death itself, so the shepherd looks for quiet or still pools where his sheep can drink without trouble.

The shepherd doesn't only feed the sheep, but he cares for them. Sheep have other needs and a shepherd is aware of them all. He works diligently to see to it that all their needs are met. A shepherd will regularly shear his sheep to remove excess wool. Often the wool has accumulated mud and dirt, insects and even manure. It is best for its health that these things be removed.

The shepherd understands the needs of the sheep better than they do themselves. And he is always on the lookout for sheep that need personal attention. The hot sun many times affects the sheep negatively. Bugs are also a problem. They become a nuisance and distraction to the sheep. The sheep will bat their heads against trees and rocks when bugs are tormenting them. They have a difficult time calming down. The shepherd rubs the sheep down with oil to keep the bugs away. In Jesus' day, the shepherds carried a supply of olive oil in a ram's horn to care for the sheep in special times of need. A shepherd is attentive to their wounds. Thorns, scratches, scrapes, cuts, and scabs are rubbed down with oil in order that they might heal.

When moving the sheep from one place to another, many sheep will fearlessly plunge into the water. Soon they are across a stream. Others enter a stream with hesitation and even alarm, so the shepherd enters the stream himself, leading the way. Some sheep miss the fording place and are carried down the river. If one is swept away, the shepherd quickly leaps into the stream and rescues it, carrying it in his arms.

The shepherd's task is to keep the flock fed, safe, and in good health. This means that the shepherd has to understand the sheep and he has to be in tune with the sounds of their cry. He knows what the sheep sound like when they are happy, and he knows what the sheep sound like when they are in need or in danger.

The shepherd is adamant about protecting his sheep. He rises early in the morning to check on the sheep, making sure they have not been harmed in the night. He protects his sheep from predators and even thieves. Shepherds would carry rods to fend off predators. The rod was used to protect the sheep from dangerous animals that were lurking, ready to attack the sheep. As the shepherd leads the sheep on long journeys between pastures he uses a staff. He gently leads and guides the sheep with the staff. The staff is a long stick with a hook and it is used many times as an aid to pull sheep out of a pit. When moving the flock from one range to another, the sheep often walk through dangerous valleys. The shepherd helps the sheep get through these rough spots. He also knows every safe passage and road of escape. He puts his own life at risk to protect and care for the sheep. He is willing to fight for his sheep. And he never abandons them.

Shepherds know how to restore a beaten, weary, exhausted and despondent sheep to bring refreshing and new life back to it. There are times when his task is to calm, comfort and soothe the sheep. A shepherd sees to it that his sheep are well fed, well cared for, well protected and in good health at all costs. The role of the shepherd signifies strength, authority, and power, and yet we see his gentleness in the way that he tends the sheep. The shepherd leads with such tender care. He *leads* the sheep beside the still waters. He doesn't *drive* them to the still waters.

Once again, we can see this servant type leadership modeled when we look at shepherding. It is an ultimate picture of the utmost care and concern. Gentlemen, let's *not* be the kind of men who agitate or trouble the waters around our wives. Instead, may we become shepherds who lead our wives to fresh, pure, living water because we have partaken of the pure water of the Word of God ourselves. May we become the kind of men who remove the very things that are weighty upon our wives, even carrying burdens for her when necessary. Rather than being the source of irritation, let's become the kind of men who actually remove irritants, along with anything else that would serve to compromise her overall good and total health. May we be shepherds who guard our wives against danger and keep her safe from harm. And may we protect her at all costs. May we be willing to lay down our lives for the woman whom God has entrusted to us. Let's be the kind of shepherd-leaders who are willing to fight her enemies. May we rescue her when she needs rescuing. May we carry her when she needs to be carried. May we be the kind of husband who knows our wife's needs better than she knows them herself. Let's become *determined* that we will not be the one who creates a wound within her heart, but instead we will be the one who brings healing to her brokenness. Let's shepherd her heart.

In 1 Peter 5:2-4, we find instructions given to the spiritual leaders:

> "Shepherd the flock of God which is among you, **serving** as overseers, not by compulsion but **willingly**, not for dishonest gain but **eagerly**; nor as being lords over those entrusted to you, but **being examples** to the flock, and when the Chief Shepherd appears, you will receive the crown of glory that does not fade away." (NKJV)

The Message Bible puts it like this:

> "**Care for** God's flock **with all the diligence** of a shepherd. Not because you have to, but **because you want to please God**. Not calculating what you can get out of it, but acting spontaneously. Not bossily telling others what to do, but **tenderly showing them the way.**"

These scriptures spell out just how to care for those entrusted to our leadership. The Amplified Bible Classic edition breaks it down the best when it says, "Tend (nurture, guard, guide, and fold) the flock of God that is [your responsibility], not by coercion or constraint, but willingly; not dishonorably motivated by the advantages and profits [belonging to the office], but eagerly and cheerfully; **not domineering [as arrogant, dictatorial, and overbearing persons] over those in your charge, but by being examples (patterns and models of Christian living**) to the flock." (emphasis is the author's)

As husbands, we are shepherds in our marriages and homes. We are, according to scripture, the leader or the head. We now have a really great picture of what this position looks like. Before we move on, let's take a look at the twenty-third Psalm, verses 1-6:

> [1]The Lord is my Shepherd [to feed, guide, and shield me], I shall not lack.

² He makes me lie down in [fresh, tender] green pastures; He leads me beside the still and restful waters.

³ He refreshes and restores my life; He leads me in the paths of righteousness [uprightness and right standing with Him—not for my earning it, but] for His name's sake.

⁴ Yes, though I walk through the [deep, sunless] valley of the shadow of death, I will fear or dread no evil, for You are with me; Your rod [to protect] and Your staff [to guide], they comfort me.

⁵ You prepare a table before me in the presence of my enemies. You anoint my head with oil; my [brimming] cup runs over.

⁶ Surely only goodness, mercy, and unfailing love shall follow me all the days of my life, and through the length of my days the house of the Lord [and His presence] shall be my dwelling place. (AMP)

What kind of shepherd is Jesus and what kind of example does He leave us?

He is the Good Shepherd who sees to it that our needs are met. He leads us to places of real rest. He restores our very souls and heals our brokenness. He leads us in paths of righteousness. He provides security for us and we need not fear the valleys that we walk through in our lives. He protects us from evil. He doesn't abandon us or bail out when the going gets tough. Instead, He remains with us. His very presence comforts us. He blesses us right in the midst of our enemies. And He anoints us with His oil, making us fit for this role of ours.

Here are some things that we can ponder as we get ready to pray:

1. Have I been in tune with the cry of my wife's heart?

2. Do I give her personal attention when she is in need of it?

3. How can I, in some way, bring refreshing and rest to her when she is weary and overwhelmed?

4. How can I be an instrument of healing and restoration to every bruised, injured, and broken place of her heart?

5. How can I shepherd her heart?

PRAYER

Lord, thank you for Your care, Your provision, and Your protection over me. You are the Good Shepherd. Thank you for giving me an example that I can follow. I can lead well because You are equipping me to do just that. Continue to anoint me and make me fit for this role. Let me lead according to Your will. Strengthen and empower me to be a spiritual leader in my marriage and my home. Grow me in these areas and give me a shepherd's heart.

HUSBANDS STEP UP YOUR GAME: LEAD. LOVE. BUILD. FIGHT.

DAY 7

I LEAD WITH PURPOSE

"For the husband is the head of the wife, as also Christ is head of the church; and He is the Savior of the body." – Ephesians 5:23 (NKJV)

The Bible uses the word "head" in Ephesians chapter 5 when it speaks to the leadership role of a husband. It is the Greek word "kephale" and it means to seize and to take hold of. It's time for the men of God to step up and seize their opportunity to lead. It is time that we take hold of the principles of God and lead well. Our wives are truly gifts to us. We have been privileged and honored to lead them.

We can go back to the book of Genesis and see how God created the heavens and the earth; the sky, sun, moon, stars, planets, land and seas. He made all the creatures of the earth. He spoke, and it was! Then He created man. He created man in His image and in His likeness. Man was set apart in that way from all other created things. The Lord God formed man from the dust of the earth and breathed the breath of life into his nostrils and man became a living soul.

Man was made for God's glory. And God recognized that it was not good for man to be alone. He was determined to provide a helpmate for him. God went to work and brought all of the living creatures before man to name them. As magnificent as everything was that God had created, there wasn't anything that could truly satisfy man. When God looked upon all that He had created, He said that it was very good. But none of these very good things were sufficient for curing man's loneliness or meeting his deeper needs. So, God seeing that there was a need, created woman. She was an answer to the need. She was that one thing that was missing. She was more satisfying than any other created thing that was given to the man. She fulfilled a need within the entire picture of all that had been created. Finally, something, someone…suitable. Here is the account:

> "And the Lord God said, "It is not good that man should be alone; I will make him a helper comparable to him." Out of the ground the Lord God formed every beast of the field and every bird of the air, and brought them to Adam to see what he would call them. And whatever Adam called each living creature, that was its name. So Adam gave names to all cattle, to the birds of the air, and to every beast of the field. But for Adam there was not found a helper comparable to him. And the Lord God caused a deep sleep to fall on Adam, and he slept; and He took one of his ribs, and closed up the flesh in its place. Then the rib which the Lord God had taken from man He made into a woman, and He brought her to the man. And Adam said: "This is now bone of my bones and flesh of my flesh; she shall be called Woman, because she was taken out of Man." Therefore a man shall leave his father and mother and be joined to his wife, and they shall become one flesh."
> – Genesis 2:18-24 (NKJV)

God Himself said that it wasn't good for the man to be alone. It wasn't best. It wasn't beneficial. So, God created that woman just for him and presented her to him as a gift. She was taken from his side to be his counterpart, his companion, and his helper. She was formed and fashioned in such a unique way when compared to the rest of creation. It was as if God was saving the very best for last. She was an answer. She was a gift. She was the only created thing that had the capacity to capture and hold his heart.

Do you think of your wife as an answer and a gift?

Do you think of your role as her husband as a privilege and an honor?

Proverbs 18:22 says, "**He who finds a wife finds a good thing**, and obtains favor from the Lord." (NKJV)

The word "good" here is the Hebrew word "tob". It means good in the widest sense. It translates as "best, better, bountiful, pleasure, precious, well-favored and a benefit."

Your wife is not inferior. She is precious. She is so special and so precious that God requires you to handle her with special care. She is your treasure. She is more valuable than the finest of jewels. Her value is beyond measure. She is a blessing from God to you. She adds to your life. She is not taking something away from you, but she adds to you. She is a testimony to God's favor upon your life.

> "He who finds a wife finds a good thing, **and obtains favor from the Lord**." – Proverbs 18:22 (Emphasis is the author's)

One of the greatest things a man can ever receive from the Lord is favor. It is God's favor that changes everything in the life of a man. Favor can be described as the demonstration of God's delight in a person. It is tangible, evidential and provable approval of the Lord toward a person.

The word "favor" in Proverbs 18:22 is the Hebrew word "ratson" and it means pleasure, delight, and acceptance. It is related to the word "ratsah" meaning to be pleased with and to pardon.

Matthew Henry has this to say about Proverbs 18:22 and the finding of a wife: "He has found that which will not only contribute more than anything to his comfort in this life, but will forward him in the way to heaven. God is to be acknowledged in it with thankfulness; it is a token of his favour, and a happy pledge of further favours; it is a sign that God delights in a man to do him good and has mercy in store for him; for this, therefore, God must be sought unto."

John Wesley insists that a man "obtains her not by his own diligence, but by God's good providences."

Ah, God was thinking of your good when He gave you your wife.

> "Now the Lord God said, "It is not good (beneficial) for the man to be alone; I will make him a helper [one who balances

him – a counterpart who is] suitable and complementary for him." – Genesis 2:18 (AMP)

Suitable means precisely adapted to a particular situation, need, or circumstance; fitting. She is just right for you! God created that woman to help you become a well-balanced man. Your wife was given to you to complement you. She is your helper in the sense that she is called alongside you to help you become all that you are called to be and to do. The word "help" means to give assistance, to lend strength to or means to affecting a purpose, to help forward, to advance by assistance, to aid in completing a design, and to enable to surmount. It translates as an aid, a backer, an advocate and a champion. Are you getting this, Man of God? Your wife is valuable to you.

According to 1 Corinthians 11:7, she is your glory. According to Proverbs 12:4, she is your crown! You must treat her accordingly.

Matthew Henry also says that "the duty of husbands is to *love* their wives for without this they would abuse their superiority and headship."

Leading and loving must go hand in hand!

"Husbands, love your wives, just as Christ also loved the church and gave Himself for her" – Ephesians 5:25 (NKJV)

The truth is that your leadership role and all that goes along with it may seem like a duty and an obligation without cultivating this love that Ephesians 5:25 speaks of. Without this kind of appreciation and love, it is possible that your responsibilities to her may seem burdensome. What a tragedy this would be, for truly your wife is a treasure and a gift to you.

"Headship is a position of strength and authority, but it is to be a resemblance of Christ's authority over the church. Christ's authority is exercised over the church for the saving of her from evil, and the supplying of her with everything good for her. In like manner should the husband be employed for the protection and comfort of his spouse; and therefore

she should the more cheerfully submit herself unto him. A husband reckless of these obligations virtually ceases to have a claim on the subjection of the wife and family."
– Matthew Henry

This is some hard truth right here. On the wife's part, she is to submit to the husband's leadership, but just what kind of leadership have we been expecting our wives to submit to?

Ephesians 5:22 speaks to the wife, "Wives, submit to your own husbands, as to the Lord."

When talking to women who are having a difficult time with the idea of submitting to their husbands, there are always good reasons for their struggle. For one, it is hard to submit to the leadership of someone who you do not trust or a man that has taken no care. Many women make this statement: "I would gladly submit to a man who loves me like Christ loves the church."

"If it should be seen hard for the wife to be in subjection, the spirit of love, Christ-like love, on the part of the husband makes the duty easy. Christ did not merely pit the Church, or merely desire her good, but loved her; her image was stamped on his heart, and her name graven on his hands, he desired to have her for his companion, longing for a return of her affection, for the establishment of sympathy between her and him. And he gave himself for her, showing her that her happiness and welfare were dearer to him than his own- the true test of deep, real love." – Matthew Henry

Deep, real love.

These two roles, leadership and subjection, work together. The husband provides the kind of leadership that the wife gladly follows. And her subjection is a wonderful response to the way that her husband loves her. It is "an abundant return for that love of the husband which God has made her due."

Leading well includes loving well. And a man who leads well also knows where he is headed. Let's take a quick look at this idea of submission on the part of our wives before we move on.

Submission

The prefix *sub* means to be under. Therefore, submission means to be under one and the same mission. A mission, by the way, is a calling or an important assignment.

A wife, then, virtually is being asked to bring herself under one and the same mission as her husband.

God has a calling upon your life. He has important assignments for you. Do you know what those assignments might be? What is your calling? What is your God-given purpose? What is it that you sense God is calling you to be and to do? Do you know? If not, begin to pray about that. Ask God to show you specifically. And then share that with your wife.

A man needs a purpose. He needs a vision and a cause that is greater than himself. Men want their lives to count for something. They want to make a difference. It is important for a man to know just what he is designed and called to do.

God has a plan and a purpose for you and your wife individually. And He also has a common purpose for you as a married couple. God has a calling for you as one. Find out just what that purpose is and then lead her and love her in a way that glorifies God and causes you both to accomplish every one of His purposes and assignments.

Seize and take hold of your role as the head. Know where you are going and run!

PRAYER

Lord, I thank You for Your favor upon my life. Thank You for the gift of my wife. Thank You for the privilege and the honor that You have given me to lead her. Help me to apply all that

You have been showing me concerning the way that You would have me lead. Take my marriage to new places in You. Don't let us miss what You have for us. Begin even now to stir my heart for the very things that You have created and called me to be and to do. Deposit within me a great sense of Your purposes for our life together as a married couple. Speak to me about the mission and assignment that You have for me and for my marriage. Lead me as I lead my wife and my family. Help me to lead well and love like Christ. In Jesus' name, Amen.

1 Corinthians 9:26 – "So I run with purpose in every step." (NLT)

LOVE

"May the Master take you by the hand and lead you along
the path of God's love and Christ's endurance."
– 2 Thessalonians 3:5 (MSG)

HUSBANDS STEP UP YOUR GAME: LEAD. LOVE. BUILD. FIGHT.

DAY 8

I IMITATE CHRIST IN THE WAY I LOVE MY BRIDE

"Husbands, love your wives, just as Christ also loved the church and gave Himself for her." – Ephesians 5:25 (NKJV)

Love your wife. Well, that should be easy, right? After all, you married that woman because you were in love and you began your life of love together, loving her the way only you know how. The only problem with that is that God never said, "Husbands, love your wives as only you know how. Love your wives your way." Quite to the contrary, God tells husbands to love their wives His way. And a husband will never truly be able to love his wife *just as Christ loved the church* until he really understands the love of Christ. This week we need to begin taking a closer look at the love of Christ that we might imitate His love, the love He has for His bride.

Chapter 5 of Ephesians begins with these words, "Therefore be imitators of God as dear children. And walk in love, as Christ also has loved us and given Himself for us, an offering and a sacrifice to God for a sweet-smelling aroma." (verses 1-2 NKJV)

Imitators. The word "imitator" is the word mimētēs in the original Greek language. This word is actually from the related word mimeomai, from which we get the word mimic or mime. We are to imitate or mimic Christ in the way that we love.

> "Therefore be imitators of God [copy Him and follow His example], as well-beloved children [imitate their father]." – Ephesians 5:1 (AMP)

59

Many men that I talk to today did not really have any good examples modeled in front of them as they were growing up. Some have come out of dysfunctional or broken homes. The rest of us may have grown up in good, godly homes. Whatever our background, we have all learned to love from someone. Whether we realize it or not, we have watched and learned. And we may even be consciously or unconsciously imitating those things that we have seen and experienced.

Sadly, I have had more than one young man admit to me, "I really want to be a good husband and a good father, but I don't know what that looks like." Statements like this usually come from men whose fathers abandoned their mother, or fathers who simply were not present growing up. Where do they learn? Who do they watch? What do they imitate? Like you and I, they have all done the best they know how. And when a man feels like he has done the best he knows how, yet his best is not good enough, it leaves him with a sense of failure.

The truth is we have not been left without a model or without the tools necessary to be the men of God that He calls us to be. We have a model and that model is Christ. He has left us an example to see and a blueprint to follow. In many of our cases, this means that we will need to unlearn all the wrong things and relearn all the right things. Today is the day we begin to do just that.

Here are a few questions to ponder as we get started:

Did my own father leave me an example and a model to follow when it comes to loving my wife?

What man in my life has modeled in front of me how to be a good husband?

Who and what was my teacher?

Who and what have I been imitating?

> "Watch what God does, and then you do it, like children who learn proper behavior from their parents. Mostly what God does is love you. Keep company with him and learn a life of

love. Observe how Christ loved us. His love was not cautious but extravagant. He didn't love in order to get something from us but to give everything of himself to us. Love like that."
– Ephesians 5:1-2 (MSG)

Extravagant. That is what God's love is. 1 John 3:1 says, "See what great love the Father has lavished on us, that we should be called children of God!" (NIV)

God has a great love for you and for me, and the Bible tells us that He lavishes it upon us. To lavish means to give unsparingly. It is a love that is given in an unrestrained way. To lavish means to shower, pour or heap. It is excessive, immoderate, bountiful, and profuse! It is rich and elaborate. To lavish means to bestow something in generous or extravagant quantities. God's love is more than enough.

The Amplified Bible says, "See what [an incredible] quality of love the Father has given [shown, bestowed on] us."

His love is one of incredible quality and quantity.

In Ephesians 3:18, Paul prayed that the Ephesians would truly grasp just "how wide, and long, and high, and deep" the love of God truly is. It is a love that goes beyond ordinary parameters. Do we really understand the scope of His love for us?

Romans 5:8 tells us that while we were yet sinners, while we were yet God's enemies, He loved us and gave Himself for us. Before we demonstrated any kind of love towards Him, He demonstrated His love for us. When we were unlovable, He loved us. When we didn't deserve His love, He didn't hold His love back from us. Instead, He lavished it upon us. His feelings and His emotions did not hold Him on that cross. Neither should our feelings and emotions alone dictate to us just how we will love our wives or under what circumstances we will love them. We must love our wives with the love of Christ, the kind of love that is unrelenting, the kind of love that just doesn't give up.

Romans 8:38-40 tells us more about this great love of Christ: "neither death, nor life, nor angels, nor principalities, nor things present and threatening, nor things to come, nor powers, nor height nor depth, nor any other created thing, will be able to separate us from the [unlimited] love of God, which is in Christ Jesus our Lord." (AMP)

Nothing can separate us from the love of God; "Not trouble, not hard times, not hatred, not hunger, not homelessness, not bullying threats, not backstabbing, not even the worst sins listed in Scripture." "I'm absolutely convinced that nothing—nothing living or dead, angelic or demonic, today or tomorrow, high or low, thinkable or unthinkable— absolutely *nothing* can get between us and God's love because of the way that Jesus our Master has embraced us." – Romans 8:35, 38-39 (MSG)

Now that is an incredible love! Nothing can separate us from it, not even past sins and failures. Nothing we have done or *not* done can separate us from the love of God. His love is not earned or even deserved. It is a free gift. He loves us with a high quality, extravagant, perfect, unconditional, unfailing love. What might happen today if you made a commitment to love your wife in this same manner?

Let's take a second look at our key scripture today:

> "Watch what God does, and then you do it, like children who learn proper behavior from their parents. Mostly what God does is love you. Keep company with him and learn a life of love. Observe how Christ loved us. His love was not cautious but extravagant. **He didn't love in order to get something from us** but to give everything of himself to us. Love like that." – Ephesians 5:1-2 MSG (emphasis is the author's)

Christ's love is a love that is marked by His giving, the giving of Himself. The world's way says, "Take. Take. Take." God's way says, "Give. Give. Give."

How did Christ love the church? His greatest demonstration of love to the church appeared in His giving of Himself unto death for it. The Bible tells us that there is no greater love than a love that lays down its life for another. It is not a self-serving love but a self-denying love. Loving your bride first and loving her best brings out the ultimate good for you both.

"Husbands, go all out in your love for your wives, exactly as Christ did for the church—a love marked by giving, not getting. Christ's love makes the church whole. His words evoke her beauty. Everything he does and says is designed to bring the best out of her, dressing her in dazzling white silk, radiant with holiness. And that is how husbands ought to love their wives. They're really doing themselves a favor—since they're already "one" in marriage." – Ephesians 5:25-28 (MSG)

Do yourself a favor. Go all out in your love for your wife. Let it be a love marked by giving.

PRAYER

Lord, thank You for the way that You love me and thank You for the model You have left me to follow as I love my bride like You have loved Yours. Continue to give me a fresh revelation of this love that I might truly imitate it. Teach me how to love Your way. I make a new commitment today to love my wife with an extravagant love. Light within me a greater, richer, and deeper love for my wife. Fill us both anew with love one for another and may every difficulty that we press through together only serve to strengthen and increase the love that we have. Bring forth an overflow of love in our marriage and let that overflow begin with me.

HUSBANDS STEP UP YOUR GAME: LEAD. LOVE. BUILD. FIGHT.

DAY 9

I AM A FORGIVING AND COMPASSIONATE SPOUSE

"Behold what manner of love the Father hath bestowed upon us."
– 1 John 3:1 (NKJV)

This week we are taking some time to do just that. We are taking a fresh look at just what kind of love He extends to us that we might imitate this love in our marriages. We are walking in our role as husbands when we love His way.

"And walk in love, as Christ also has loved us and given Himself for us, an offering and a sacrifice to God for a sweet-smelling aroma." – Ephesians 5:2 (NKJV)

Chapter 5 of Ephesians opens up by telling us to walk in love. The word for "love" here is the word *agapē*. It translates as affection or benevolence, a love feast. A feast of love! Now, that gets my attention. Thayer's Bible Dictionary defines *agapē* as brotherly love, affection, and goodwill. The rest of the verse tells us *how* we can mimic this kind of love: "And walk in love, **as Christ also has loved us and given Himself for us.**" Christ's love is a love marked by giving. He willingly gave Himself for our sake as He was nailed to a cross to bleed and die for the purpose of our souls. Verses 26 and 27 reveal more about His purposes in the giving of Himself.

"That He might sanctify and cleanse her with the washing of water by the word that He might present her to Himself a glorious church, not having spot or wrinkle or any such

65

thing, but that she should be holy and without blemish."
– (Ephesians 5:26-27)

Christ's purpose in laying down His life was the sanctifying of His bride. His desire was to one day present her as a glorious church free from the stain of sin. He laid down his life in order that she might be presented as holy and without blame!

Without blame.

Christ took the blame, didn't he? Now that is extravagant. He was without sin, yet He took the blame. He took our sin, our guilt, our shame, our shortcomings, our faults, and our failures. He took the blame! He didn't deserve it, yet not only did He take the blame, but He also took the penalty that was due. This is the kind of giving and taking that we see Jesus doing; giving Himself and taking our blame.

Christian husbands, have we become blame shifters or blame takers?

Unlike Christ who was innocent, many times we are not innocent. We really are to blame for the offenses and issues within our marriage relationship, and yet we refuse to take what's rightfully ours. "Don't blame me!" — We don't want to be wrong about anything. Even when we are indeed at fault, we are guilty and still not willing to own it.

This is not what Christ modeled. Bridegroom Jesus laid down a different blueprint for us. His plan looks a bit different, a whole lot different. As husbands, not only are we to take ownership of our own faults, living responsibly, but we are to go a step further and take up or carry hers, that she might be presented blameless before God. "I love her so much, God, I will take all the blame! Put it on me!"

Isn't that what Jesus did?

Now that is extravagant love. Are you willing to take the blame? Stop putting all the blame on her, the blame that doesn't belong to her, and even the blame that technically does.

This sanctifying work that Christ did by the laying down of His life was about freeing His bride from sin. The word "sanctify" in verse

26 means to purify internally by the renewing of the soul. Christ did the most unselfish thing that He could, not to advance Himself but to advance His bride. Her condition and her well-being were on His mind. This sanctifying work was about saving her, healing her, and making her whole. Christ demonstrated His total devotion to His bride by the laying down of His own life.

Albert Barnes says this about these very important scriptures: "**That he might sanctify**—The great object of the Redeemer was to purify and save the church. The meaning here is, that a husband is to manifest similar love toward his wife, and a similar desire that she should be prepared to "walk before him in white".

Christ's immediate object was to cleanse His bride from the guilt and power of sin. His heart was to rescue, restore and develop her character. He made the ultimate sacrifice with her highest good in mind. And according to verse 26, the purifying agent is the Word of God.

> "Husbands, love your wives [seek the highest good for her and surround her with a caring, unselfish love], just as Christ also loved the church and gave Himself up for her, so that He might sanctify the church, having cleansed her **by the washing of water with the word [of God]**." – (Amplified Bible)

Are you willing to demonstrate your total devotion to your bride, doing everything within your power to see to it that she is washed with the Word of God that one day you might present yourself along with her to God without spot, wrinkle, or blemish?

Do you need to make a brand-new commitment today to follow Christ's example in the way that you love your spouse?

Samuele Bacchiocchi, the author of *The Marriage Covenant*, says that many times this kind of commitment looks a lot like the way of the cross in this way, "growth in our marital commitment often takes place through deaths and resurrections. There are times in our marital relationship when communication becomes very difficult, if not impossible. Hurt, hostility, and resentment seem to prevail. Yet, as we learn by God's grace to put to death and to bury all such ill-feelings, out of that dying, new life comes in our relationship."

Man of God, do you need new life to come into your marriage relationship? What is it that you need to put to death and bury today? Is it your own selfish ways? Is it something that you have been holding against your wife?

> "The duty of husbands is to love their wives." "The love of Christ to the church is proposed as an example of this, which love of his is a sincere, a pure, an ardent, and constant affection, and that notwithstanding the imperfections and failures that she is guilty of." – Matthew Henry

Are you willing to be a compassionate and forgiving spouse?

Christ took the blame upon Himself and extended forgiveness to His bride. And the truth is that you and I look most like Christ when we forgive. To forgive is to give up a debt, to lay it aside, to let go of it and to send it away.

Release your wife from all blame and the imperfections and failures that she is guilty of. Release her from any guilt whatsoever, that she might draw near to both you and the Lord with a cleansed conscience. Let this same object be within you; the growth and development of her character and the well-being of her soul. Be willing to make sacrifices for her ultimate good.

PRAYER

> Lord, I am the head, which comes with responsibility and accountability before You. I take full responsibility. Not only will I lead well, but I will love well. Help me to love like You love, Lord. Help me to crucify my own selfish ways that my love might be marked by giving and the giving of myself. Help me to break any cycles of blame-shifting in my life. Cause me to become a forgiving and compassionate spouse.

I am willing to demonstrate my total devotion to my bride in the way that I love her and from this day forward I will love her Your way, rather than my own. I am ready to make every and any sacrifice necessary for her ultimate good. Cause new life to come into my marriage relationship now, in Jesus' Name.

DAY 10

I NOURISH AND CHERISH MY WIFE

"Husbands, love your wives [seek the highest good for her and surround her with a caring, unselfish love], just as Christ also loved the church and gave Himself up for her." – Eph. 5:25 (AMP)

Christ's object in the giving of Himself was to save His bride from evil, remove guilt, impart new life, develop her and bring out the best in her. In what ways can we bring out the best in our wives as we learn to love like Christ? The Expositor's Bible Commentary says that we have great influence in these very things:

> "The perfection of the wife's character will be to the religious husband one of the dearest objects in life. He will desire for her that which is highest and best, as for himself. He is put in charge of a soul more precious to him than any other, over which he has an influence incomparably, great."

> "And this kind of love that a husband demonstrates toward his own wife is marked by self-devotion, not self-satisfaction. It's strength and authority it uses as material for sacrifice and instruments of service, not as prerogatives of pride or titles to enjoyment. Let this mind be in you, O husband, toward your wife, which was also in Christ Jesus, who was meek and lowly in heart, counting it His honour to serve and His reward to save and bless." (Expositor's Bible Commentary)

It is a caring and unselfish love that a husband ought to imitate, and truly this kind of love brings out the best in his wife. The writer of Ephesians chapter five relates this type of caring to the kind of care one would take towards his very own body.

> "So husbands ought to love their own wives as their own bodies; he who loves his wife loves himself. For no one ever hated his own flesh, but nourishes and cherishes it, just as the Lord does the church." (Verses 28-29 NKJV)

Nourish and Cherish

One of your greatest opportunities that comes with marriage is that of nourishing and cherishing your spouse. A husband should love his wife in the same way he loves himself. He should regard her as one with himself and treat her accordingly. Is a man hungry, tired, sick, suffering? How will he care for himself? He will do what is necessary to make himself healthy and whole.

The word "nourish" in verse 29 is the word *ektrepho* and it means to pamper, to feed and to strengthen. It also means to rear up to maturity. This word "nourish" seems to imply both sustenance physically and spiritually. And the word "cherish," *thalpo* in the original Greek language, translates as to cherish with tender love and to foster with care.

First, the two expressions together speak of providing food and clothing. The sense here is that the husband provides for her and guards her against exposure to want. The husband demonstrates tender concern for the needs of his wife just as Christ does the church.

1 Timothy 5:8 says, "But if any provide not for his own, and specially for those of his own house, he hath denied the faith, and is worse than an infidel." Providing for our wife's needs is an important part of our role as a Christian husband. Ephesians 5:29 seems to imply that neglecting to provide for her needs violates the very laws of nature itself.

As men, we are quick to satisfy our own need for nourishment. We rarely neglect our own bodies. A man values himself. He takes care of his own body, guarding and protecting it from injury, pain, suffering, discomfort, and lack, feeding and nourishing it. He nourishes and cherishes it, some men more than others. Many men will spend hours at the gym building and sculpting their bodies. They lift, run, swim, and work those bodies out. Health and fitness are important to them. Today, men are eating clean, putting only the best food and beverages into their bodies. They are health conscious and they are taking extra care with their diets, avoiding harmful chemicals, hormones, bad fats, and limiting sugars. They are eating more protein, drinking plenty of water and even *green* shakes. They want to feel better and live longer. The younger male generation today waxes their eyebrows and gets manicures and pedicures.

As I watched my boys go through their teen years and even their twenties, I realized that they had more product taking up space in our bathrooms than their mother did; hair products, shampoo, conditioner, hair gel, paste and putty, skin products, beard grooming razors, trimmers, combs, and beard oil, teeth whitener and the list goes on. They take care of their bodies and dress them in only the best clothing. They have more shoes than any woman that I know. I have never seen men take better care of themselves than they do today. Our care for our wife's needs should be just as acute. We are to labor to provide what she needs and even strive to provide nourishment for her soul.

These two words used here in verse 29, nourish (ektrepho) and cherish (thalpo), provide a unique picture of caring that goes beyond the simple provisions of food, clothing, and basic necessities. After all, Christ's care and concern for His bride goes beyond the simple necessities of life. He constantly nourishes His bride, protects it from harm, hurt, and promotes her comfort and welfare. To "nourish" also translates as "to rear up to maturity". This is not in the sense as the rearing up or training up of a child. Instead, it is the kind of responsibility that a husband takes for his wife's ongoing spiritual, mental, and emotional growth. She is in his care. And he cares for her better than he cares for himself. A love with selfish interest will do anything that it believes will advance itself, but a love with unselfish interest makes its ambition to advance her. What are we doing to assure that our wives are advancing in every area?

The Amplified version of Ephesians 5:25 puts it like this, "Husbands, love your wives [seek the highest good for her and surround her with a caring, unselfish love] just as Christ loved the church and gave Himself up for her."

A Caring, Unselfish Love

Are you taking good care of your wife? What kind of love and care have you been surrounding her with?

We have a large, green, thriving plant in our living room. Its leaves spread out in different directions and cover the stand it sits upon. The leaves are dark green, and the plant is beautiful to look at. How has it become the flourishing plant that it is? It is that way because it is watered, fed, and placed in the proper light to give it what it needs to thrive.

Your relationship with your wife is the same way. Water it. Give it nourishment and make sure you place it in the light of the gospel so real, genuine growth can burst forth. Surround her with caring, unselfish love.

Nourish and cherish your wife. To "cherish" means to protect and care for lovingly, to hold something dear, treasure, prize, adore, dote on, be devoted to, respect, esteem, admire, and to feel or show tenderness and great affection. What a great picture of the tender love and care that husbands are to demonstrate towards their wives.

> "So husbands ought to love their own wives as their own bodies; he who loves his wife loves himself. For no one ever hated his own flesh, but nourishes and cherishes it, just as the Lord does the church." – Ephesians 5:28-29 (NKJV)

"**And he is the Saviour of the body**—that is, of the church, represented as "his body;" The idea here seems to be, that as Christ gave himself to save his body, the church; as he practiced self-denial and made it an object of intense solicitude to preserve that church, so ought the husband to manifest a similar solicitude to make his wife happy, and to save her from want, affliction, and pain. He ought to regard himself as her natural protector; as bound to anticipate and provide for her needs; as under obligation to comfort her in trial, even as Christ does the church. What a beautiful illustration of the spirit which a husband should manifest is the care which Christ has shown for his "bride," the church!" – Albert Barnes

PRAYER

Lord, help me to demonstrate such care. Speak to me about how I can seek my wife's highest good. If I have influence in the development of her character, then let me use that influence that I might see the very best come out of her. There is so much in my wife and I desire to see her reach her highest potential. Forgive me, Lord, for any area where I have neglected her. Show me how I might bring nourishment to my wife not only physically, but emotionally and spiritually as well. I vow today to surround her with caring, unselfish love. I vow to show tenderness and great affection in the way that I love her. I pray that You would cause my wife, our relationship, and marriage to absolutely flourish like never before as You teach me daily to walk in this love.

DAY 11

MY WIFE IS MY PRIORITY

"So husbands ought to love their own wives as their own bodies;
he who loves his wife loves himself. For no one ever hated his
own flesh, but nourishes and cherishes it, just as the Lord does
the church. For we are members of His body, of His flesh and His
bones. **"For this reason a man shall leave his father and mother**
and be joined to his wife, and the two shall become one flesh."
This is a great mystery, but I speak concerning Christ and the
church. Nevertheless let each one of you in particular so love his
own wife as himself, and let the wife see that she respects her
husband." – Ephesians 5:28-33 (NKJV) emphasis is the author's

From the beginning, a man leaves his father and mother and is
joined to his wife. Likewise, the woman leaves her mother and father
and is joined to her husband. To leave implies a priority change.
A husband's relationship to his wife is now preferred to all others,
even the relationships that have possibly been the most important
relationships in his life up until the time of marriage.

Some translations of Ephesians 5:31 use the words "cleave" and "is
yoked together". Cleaving is better described as gluing or so firmly
adhering to one another that nothing and no one can separate them.
The two are no longer separate. They do not continue to have separate
interests but act as one. To cleave means "to cling to, to pursue
hard after, and to follow closely." It means "to be united closely in
interest and affection; to adhere with strong attachment, to be stitched
together, to keep close, to stick with or stay with."

Leaving, Cleaving, and Being Yoked Together

Upon marrying, a man needs to understand that a priority change has taken place. He cannot allow other relationships to come between himself and his bride. This includes relationships with his own family. I have watched many times as parents, particularly mothers, struggle to release a son, wanting to continue having a say in his decisions, and in some extreme cases continue to have some level of control in his life. This causes havoc in the marriage relationship. Mom must except that your priority is now your wife. Your wife must be first. The apron string must be cut and if necessary it must be cut by you. Nobody wants to upset Mom. After all, she will always be an important part of your life, but it is important that she understands that you are a grown man who is ready to take charge of his own life. A shift has taken place. Your wife is now your priority and she wants to be number one. That means she comes first above your relationship with all others including your buddies…all of them. This includes the amount of time spent with friends versus the amount of time spent with her. She is now your top priority. There has been a change from the single life to the married life.

It is amazing how many marriage relationships are quickly in trouble due to other relationships in a man's life. Husbands, we cannot allow this to happen. Leaving, cleaving, and being joined together is vital to the success of a marriage.

To be joined together is better translated as "to be yoked together." It is the word or term "suzeugnumi" in the original Greek language and it is a picture of the oxen being yoked together in the plow where each must pull equally in order to bring it forward. Being joined together is being so closely tied and united that a husband and wife are pulling equally together in all the concerns of life. They are moving together as one. Their hearts are set on the same mission.

A husband and wife are no longer focused on their own wants, desires, and needs, but now have a brand-new focus. That focus must become one. That is not to say they will not still have different likes, interests, and desires. Of course, they will. But clearly, priorities

78

have changed. There is a brand-new focus. They never put their own desires first above their spouse with no regard for them. Two people continuing to pursue their own separate, self-centered, or self-seeking desires will quickly be in conflict. Two people remaining separate in the marriage relationship will be in a constant state of conflict. Conflict breeds division, not unity. And we know that a house divided against itself cannot stand.

I like what Jack Hayford says about the vital unity between a husband and wife:

> "From the beginning, God's heart to build a dwelling place for Himself in the Earth is seen in His creation of man and woman—together, the foundation of the house of the Lord. Through the two of them together, He intended to live and reveal Himself in the world. Through them, God intended to manifest His character and authority (image), express His dominion over the [e]arth, display His indisputable power over the works of darkness, and subdue His archenemy, Satan. The first man and woman were a microcosm of the church, signaling that God's glory would forever be seen in the [e]arth through the combined expression of male and female. Now, as then, God's blessing—His promise of success—is upon our unity."

This oneness, this unity in our marriages, is so important. Hayford states that God's promise of success is upon our unity. I believe that! I am also reminded of Psalm 133:1-3, which says, "Behold, how good and how pleasant it is for brethren to dwell together in unity! It is like the precious oil upon the head, running down on the beard, the beard of Aaron, running down on the edge of his garments. It is like the dew of Hermon, descending upon the mountains of Zion; for there the Lord commanded the blessing – life forevermore." (NKJV)

There, in the place of unity, the Lord commands the blessing. Not only does He command blessings and promises of success upon the marriage as you both become one, but He desires to reveal Himself to the world through the relationship of a husband and wife. If this is the case (and it is), then our greatest mission as a married couple is to reflect Jesus Christ. It is to put Jesus on display. There is a much bigger picture here. Marriage is a small thing that is part of a bigger picture. We must come to the realization that our Christian marriages are a picture of Christ and the Church. The Christian marriage is a portrait of Christ's deep, enduring, and sacrificial love for His people. If we are to be that kind of image bearer, it is time to get it together and present an accurate picture to the world. It is time to once and for all truly become one with our spouse and learn to love her like Christ loves the Church.

Christ invites us into an intimate union with Him. He longs for that oneness with His bride. His life is wrapped up in her. Matthew Henry refers to this love as a "sincere, peculiar, singular, pervading love."

I remember the days when either myself or one of my buddies was in a dating relationship and they started exhibiting that love-struck, lovesick kind of behavior. We would use the term, "You are wrapped, man!" Of course, any one of us would try to deny it no matter how ridiculously apparent it was to everyone. Wrapped! That is how we should be as husbands today. We have given our whole heart to our wife and it is indeed a sincere, peculiar, singular, pervading love.

PRAYER

Lord, my love for my wife is a sincere love. My love for You is a sincere love as well and I only want to represent You with the utmost honor and respect. If my priorities are not in line in any area of my life, help me to correct that immediately. Bring a greater oneness within my relationship with my wife. Knit us and glue us together in a much stronger and sweeter way. Continue to reveal Your love to me each day, fill me with Your love each day, help me to release Your love each day and reflect it well. Command Your blessings and Your promises of success upon my marriage union, in Jesus' Name I pray.

DAY 12

MY LOVE STORY IS BUT A REFLECTION OF THE GREATEST LOVE STORY EVER TOLD

"For this reason a man shall leave his father and mother and be joined to his wife, and the two shall become one flesh."
– Ephesians 5:31 (NKJV)

Why did you get married?

What if I told you that God has a greater purpose for marriage and it goes far beyond your own intent? God ordained marriage from the very beginning (Genesis 2). He saw that it was not good for the man to be alone. He created the woman and presented her to the man as a gift. The man was overwhelmed with the blessing of his helper, his counterpart, his companion and soul mate. This bond was like no other. And in Genesis 2:24 God said to him, "Therefore a man shall leave his father and mother and be joined to his wife, and the two shall become one flesh."

Marriage was God's idea! And just like God, He had a purpose to fulfill that goes far beyond meeting the man's needs. He had much more in mind than procreation and the filling of the earth with generations to come. He had a plan that reaches outside of the man and into the world around him. It is His intent to use man in His plan of redemption. God has created you and me in His image and in His likeness. He tells us to be imitators of His Son, Bridegroom Jesus. And through our demonstration of Christ's love toward our own bride, we are ultimate witnesses.

Do you want to be used by God? Pay attention.

> "For this reason a man shall leave his father and mother and be joined to his wife, and the two shall become one flesh. This is a great mystery, but I speak concerning Christ and the church Nevertheless let each one of you in particular so love his own wife as himself, and let the wife see that she respects her husband." – Ephesians 5:31-33 (NKJV)

What is this great *mystery* that Paul speaks of in Ephesians chapter five? It is the love that Jesus has for His people, the church. And He wants to reveal this love through the relationship of a husband and a wife.

All throughout scripture we can find this language of love which refers to Christ as the Bridegroom and His church as His bride. Most Bible scholars agree that from the very beginning, marriage was designed by God to symbolize the relationship of Christ to the church.

Wait a minute—that's pretty deep. A Christian marriage is supposed to symbolize the relationship of Christ to the church? If that is the case, my wife and I have a responsibility to reflect that correctly.

In Ephesians 5:25, husbands are instructed to love their wives as Christ loved the church and gave Himself for her, redeeming and sanctifying her. We know this story well, don't we? It is the greatest love story ever told! Our sin separated us from God, but while we were yet sinners, Christ loved us and died for us. When we deserved death and Hell, He demonstrated His love for us. Christ left His father's home in Heaven and came to earth to live a sinless life so that He might redeem us. Jesus, who was without sin, paid the penalty of sin for us that we might be reconciled to God. He did something for us that we could not have done for ourselves. By laying down His life, He provided a way for us to be forgiven and one day spend eternity in Heaven with Him. Through His great sacrifice, we can be delivered and healed. Because of His death and resurrection, we can have full, meaningful, abundant life right now. All these provisions were made out of His passion and great love for us. All of these benefits we possess came through Christ's own suffering, pain, rejection, and self-sacrifice. That was His way of love, and what a beautiful love story it is.

Because of His great love, Christ laid down His life for us and verse 31 of Ephesians chapter five says, "**for this reason**, a man shall leave his father and mother and be joined together to his wife."—For what reason?—That this mystery of Christ's love for His church might be on display through our marriages.

If, indeed, our marriage was designed by God from the very beginning to model or reflect Christ's love for His church, how are we doing? Are our marriages showing the world an accurate picture?

It is God's desire to form an intimate union with His people. He desires to have such an intimate communion with us that we would become one with Him. This is the way of love, and our marriage relationships are to be a portrait of this great love!

If our marriages can be a testimony, a witness, and an image of something greater—Christ's love for His people—what kind of image bearers have we been?

If the Bridegroom's love for His bride is on display through our own marriages, does my marriage really resemble Christ's story of love?

Can the witness of our love for one another in our marriages really have an impact on a lost and dying world around us? If so, what kind of impact is it making now? Am I displaying the gospel message in my marriage?

Is my marriage representing the attitude and conduct of Christ, and does it point to something bigger—the reality of Jesus Christ's relationship to His church? Is this marriage an earthly symbol of a heavenly reality?

No wonder the enemy of our soul seeks to destroy the sanctity of marriage. No wonder he works so hard to destroy the family. His goal is to distort and pervert the symbol and type of Christ's love for His people! Marriage, therefore, must be protected.

What is my part as the husband? How do I contribute to this visible picture for all to see the love between Christ and His bride, the church? I do it by loving my bride like He loves His.

A husband fulfills a unique role. Meditating on these truths presents us with a new perspective of why we must lead and love our wives His way. It also creates an urgency about understanding and knowing the gospel better than we ever have before. We have entered into a covenant of love with our spouse and our marriages are holy.

PRAYER

Lord, You have ordained and set apart the marriage relationship from the very beginning. Not only will I protect the sanctity of my marriage, but I will strive to represent Bridegroom Jesus to the best of my ability. I am beginning to understand my unique role as a husband better than ever before. Transform my heart, Lord, in a way that causes me to become a true image bearer, that I might reflect an accurate picture to the world around me of the incredible love that You have for mankind. May my love and devotion to my bride point people to Jesus and put His love on display. I desire my marriage relationship to be a strong witness and testimony for Christ's name and His glory. Continue to speak to me about the ways in which my marriage makes an impact upon the world around me. And teach me to love my wife just as Christ has loved the church.

CHAPTER 13

I AM A COVENANT KEEPER

"Husbands, love your wives, just as Christ also loved the church and gave Himself for her." – Ephesians 5:25 (NKJV)

Marriage was instituted by God Himself. It was His idea from the very beginning to be a holy and lasting covenant. Not only did He institute this covenant, but He demonstrated to us how to keep it.

What is a covenant? The word "covenant" is a biblical word. It is of Latin origin (con venire) and it means "a coming together." It is when two or more parties come together to make a lasting and binding agreement with promises, stipulations, privileges, and responsibilities. The Old Testament uses the word covenant 280 times (berit) and this word is most accurately translated as "promise or pledge." The New Testament uses the word covenant thirty-three times (diatheke) and it most frequently means "a bond or a pact."

On your wedding day, you made a covenant with your bride in the presence of God. In many ways, your wedding ceremony itself resembled the practices of ancient covenant making.

Ancient covenants were always very solemn and serious agreements. First, everyone involved considered the agreement. The terms and conditions were outlined. They counted the cost of entering into the covenant and then responded. Almost every covenant called upon one or more witnesses. Sacrifices were almost always included. Some sort of token was exchanged as a symbol of the two individuals' desire to no longer live independently. Common tokens were things like robes, belts, or weapons. If robes were exchanged, it symbolized the putting on of each other and becoming one. It also symbolized the taking on of a new position, a new character, and a new authority.

Belts, which were a part of the armor, symbolized the giving of one's strengths and also the taking on of one's weaknesses. When weapons were exchanged as a token, it symbolized the commitment of defeating each other's enemies. The token itself was to be a seal which became the mark of the covenant, reminding both parties of the pact that bound them together as one.

Other customs of ancient covenant making included what they referred to as "the walk unto death." The two parties, or a representative from each party, would walk around the pieces of a sacrificed animal in a figure eight and then face each other. In this way, they were pledging to fulfill their obligations to keep the covenant. It was a vow unto death in order to fulfill their side of the pact. While the two parties stood in the middle of the sacrifice, each would pronounce aloud the terms of the covenant. Often a promise or blessing would be involved. It was also common to exchange names, implying an exchange of personality, character, reputation, and authority. A covenant meal was shared in celebration. The meal always included bread and wine, which represented the body and blood of the covenant partners. As they celebrated the meal, they made their concluding declaration that they would live as one. And from that day forward, others viewed them as one.

In ancient times, covenants were made between individuals, tribes, and nations. Commonly, the covenant's purpose was for protection, strength, or prosperity. These covenants were taken very seriously. There was a sacredness about the vows they took, and they were meant to be kept and not broken.

In the Word of God, we read about people making covenants with other people and most importantly, God Himself making covenants with His people. God made a covenant with Noah, Abraham, Moses, and David. And He made a covenant with His people, Israel, on Mount Sinai, one that the prophets speak of as a marriage covenant.

> "The Lord did not set his affection on you and choose you because you were more numerous than other peoples, for you were the fewest of all peoples. But it was because the

Lord loved you and kept the oath he swore to your ancestors that he brought you out with a mighty hand and redeemed you from the land of slavery, from the power of Pharaoh King of Egypt. Know therefore that the Lord your God is God; he is the faithful God, keeping his covenant of love to a thousand generations of those who love him and keep his commandments." – Deuteronomy 7:7-9 (NIV)

God made a covenant with His people and it was a covenant of love. The people didn't necessarily deserve His love though. They didn't always reciprocate it either. God, however, remained faithful to His covenant of love.

It all began on Mount Sinai. During the exodus from Egypt, God entered into a sacred relationship with His people known as a covenant (Exodus 20). The relationship established that day was more than the giving of the law or 10 Commandments. A relational bond was being established. As the prophets retell the events of Mount Sinai, they describe them in terms of a young bride being wooed by her divine bridegroom to enter into a marriage with him. (Hosea 2, 14-15, Jeremiah 2:1-2, Ezekiel 16)

> "When I passed by you again and looked upon you, indeed your time was the time of love; so I spread My wing over you and covered your nakedness. Yes, I swore an oath to you and entered into a covenant with you, and you became Mine," says the Lord God." – Ezekiel 16:18 (NKJV)

The people, however, were unfaithful and abandoned their covenant, turning to idols. Generation after generation was unfaithful, but God's love for His people was unrelenting. He continued to reveal His love to them through the prophets.

God told the prophet Hosea to marry a prostitute named Gomer and raise a family with her. In doing so, Hosea was demonstrating God's covenant love. When Gomer went after other lovers, God told Hosea to take her back and love her again. In doing so, he was acting out

God's unrelenting love, the kind of love that just doesn't stop. God was revealing Himself as a forgiving, compassionate, and loving spouse.

> "And it shall be, in that day," says the Lord, "that you will call Me 'My Husband,' and no longer call Me 'My Master.' I will betroth you to Me forever; Yes, I will betroth you to Me in righteousness and justice, in lovingkindness and mercy; I will betroth you to Me in faithfulness, and you shall know the Lord..." – Hosea 2:16,19-20 (NKJV)

The prophet Jeremiah reminded the people of their covenant relationship with God. Even though they had broken the covenant, God would remain faithful. It was a love that just would not let go. He promised to one day forgive His bride and establish a new covenant with her. This was their hope, that God Himself would restore the broken relationship, renew the covenant, and do the work of transforming their hearts.

> "Behold, the days are coming," says the Lord, "when I will make a new covenant with the house of Israel and with the house of Judah—not according to the covenant that I made with their fathers in the day that I took them by the hand to lead them out of the land of Egypt, My covenant which they broke, though I was a husband to them," says the Lord. "But this is the covenant that I will make with the house of Israel after those days," says the Lord: "I will put My law in their minds, and write it on their hearts; and I will be their God, and they shall be My people." – Jeremiah 31:31-33 (NKJV)

Through the prophet Ezekiel, God revealed Himself as a Husband wooing and winning back an unfaithful wife and reestablishing a lasting covenant with His bride.

> "Nevertheless I will remember My covenant with you in the days of your youth, and I will establish an everlasting covenant with you." "Then you shall know that I am the Lord, that you may remember and be ashamed, and never open

your mouth anymore because of your shame, when I provide you an atonement for all you have done," says the Lord God."
– Ezekiel 16:60, 62-63 (NKJV)

In the Old Testament, we can see God's plan to wed Himself to humankind in an everlasting marriage covenant, a covenant where love prevails! This beautiful love story continues to unfold and be fulfilled in the New Testament when Christ gave Himself for us as He was crucified, expressing His spousal love for us. We see the nature of His love in His complete devotion to His bride. It is Christ's total commitment in the giving of Himself in which the Christian marriage is to be founded upon.

In the New Testament, when Jesus was addressing questions about marriage, His response revealed that it is God Himself who actually joins a couple in marriage (Mark 10:5-9). He is the author and the witness (Malachi 2:13-14) of this divinely ordained union, making the marriage covenant all the more binding.

Paul followed the teaching of Jesus in Romans 7:1-3, stating that the marriage covenant is to be a lifelong covenant. In Ephesians chapter 5, Paul uses the marriage union to illustrate the covenant relationship between Christ and His bride, the church.

In the Old Testament, the relationship between God and Israel is portrayed as a marriage covenant. In the New Testament, the marriage union represents Christ's covenant of sacrificial love and oneness with the church. The picture of the marriage relationship is found throughout the Bible from beginning to end.

God has given us a model and a pattern to follow when it comes to loving our spouse and keeping our marriage vows. The most amazing thing is that He has given us, imperfect and often inconsistent men, the absolute power and ability to do just that. He has purposed that the Christian marriage would be a reflection of His divine love. Therefore, a Christian marriage is sacred. It is a holy matrimony. My marriage is a divinely ordained union. I have made a covenant of love with my wife. And I am determined to be a covenant keeper.

PRAYER

Lord, thank You for Your covenant of love that You have established with Your people. I am in a covenant relationship with You, Lord. I find great peace, assurance, and rest in knowing that You are faithful to keep Your promises to me. Even when I have been unfaithful to You, You have always remained faithful to me. To say that I am grateful for Your faithfulness does not come close to expressing to You what that means to me. To love the way that You love is not easy, but You have given me the power to do just that. And I will follow You in loving my wife in an unconditional, unrelenting way. I will love her with a love that just doesn't stop. Restore what is broken, Lord, and help me to love my wife with a total commitment in the giving of myself. Reestablish a strong and lasting covenant within my marriage. I honor my wedding vows. I will keep my every promise. Like Christ, I will be a covenant keeper.

DAY 14

I WILL NOT BE DRIVEN OFF COURSE

"May the Master take you by the hand and lead you along the path of God's love and Christ's endurance." – 2 Thess. 3:5 (MSG)

God is a covenant keeping God whose love endures forever. In our role as husbands, we are to love our bride as Christ loves His. Our continued prayer must be, "Show me this way of love, Lord, that I might walk in it!" God's love was best seen through Christ's endurance. Love and endurance are inseparable. We live in a world where the picture of "love" is often twisted. How sad it is for those who have never really known what love is, for we all long to love and be loved.

Before we move forward to the next unit, let's take a look at 1 Corinthians chapter 13, where an entire chapter is dedicated to the topic of love. And let's begin to ask the Lord to truly take us by the hand and lead us along the path of God's love and Christ's endurance.

> "If I speak in the tongues of men or of angels, but do not have love, I am only a resounding gong or a clanging cymbal. 2 If I have the gift of prophecy and can fathom all mysteries and all knowledge, and if I have a faith that can move mountains, but do not have love, I am nothing. 3 If I give all I possess to the poor and give over my body to hardship that I may boast, but do not have love, I gain nothing.

> 4 Love is patient, love is kind. It does not envy, it does not boast, it is not proud. 5 It does not dishonor others, it is not

self-seeking, it is not easily angered, it keeps no record of wrongs. [6] Love does not delight in evil but rejoices with the truth. [7] It always protects, always trusts, always hopes, always perseveres.

[8] Love never fails. But where there are prophecies, they will cease; where there are tongues, they will be stilled; where there is knowledge, it will pass away. [9] For we know in part and we prophesy in part, [10] but when completeness comes, what is in part disappears. [11] When I was a child, I talked like a child, I thought like a child, I reasoned like a child. When I became a man, I put the ways of childhood behind me. [12] For now we see only a reflection as in a mirror; then we shall see face to face. Now I know in part; then I shall know fully, even as I am fully known.

[13] And now these three remain: faith, hope and love. But the greatest of these is love." – 1 Corinthians 13:1-13 (NIV)

1 Corinthians chapter thirteen is often referred to as the love chapter. Within these verses, I see fourteen descriptions of what love really is (and what love really isn't).

Number 1: Love is patient. Other versions of this scripture use words like love *never gives up* or *love suffers long*. The idea of suffering long doesn't appeal to any of us, does it, yet Matthew Henry puts things in a good perspective for us when he says this about longsuffering:

> "It can endure evil, injury, and provocations, without being filled with resentment, indignation, or revenge. It makes the mind firm, gives it power over the angry passions, and furnishes it with a persevering patience, that shall rather wait and wish for the reformation of a brother than fly out in resentment of his conduct. It will put up with many slights and neglects from the person it loves, and wait long to see the kindly effects of such patience on him."

Albert Barnes defines suffering long like this: "Slowness to anger or passion; longsuffering, patient endurance, forbearance. It is opposed to haste; to passionate expressions and thoughts, and to irritability. It denotes the state of mind which can bear long when oppressed, provoked, calumniated, and when one seeks to injure us."

"Suffereth long" in the Greek translates as "to be long spirited and to patiently endure." Patience and endurance are developed over time. In fact, all of the following descriptions of love are developed as we grow. Verse eleven talks about that very thing.

> "When I was a child, I talked like a child, I thought like a child, I reasoned like a child; now that I have become a man, I am done with childish ways and have put them aside."
> – 1 Corinthians 13:11 (AMPC)

Children throw temper tantrums. They pout when they do not get their own way. They withhold affection when they are angry. Children by nature are very demanding. This scripture, however, is not referring to an infant or a minor. The word for childish in verse eleven is the Greek word *nēpios*, referring to an immature Christian. A Christian who grows and matures puts away or puts aside the immature things: immature speech, immature thinking, and immature reasoning or understanding. If we put all those immature things away, being done with them, we will cease from behaving like a child. After all, we are to "grow up in all things into Him who is the head – Christ." (Ephesians 4:15)

Number 2: Love suffers long and **is kind** (verse 4, NKJV)

I like what the Expositor's Bible Commentary has to say about this. "Love suffereth long, and is kind"; it reveals itself in a magnanimous bearing of injuries and in **a considerate and tender imparting of benefits**. It returns good for evil; not readily provoked by slights and wrongs, **it ever seeks to spend itself in kindnesses**." (emphasis is author's)

Men of God, let's choose to spend ourselves in kindness.

Number 3: It does not envy, or as the Amplified Bible puts it, "Love does not boil over with jealousy."

Number 4: Love is not puffed up. "It is not conceited (arrogant and inflated with pride)." (AMP)

Number 5: It does not dishonor others. "Love is not rude." (AMP)

Number 6: Love is not self-seeking. "It does not insist on its own rights or its own way." (AMP)

Number 7: Love is not easily angered. "Love does not fly off the handle." (MSG) "Love is not irritable." (ESV)

Number 8: Love keeps no record of wrongs.

Number 9: "Love does not rejoice at wrongdoing, but rejoices with the truth." (ESV)

Number 10: Love always protects. The NKJV uses the words "Love bears all things."

This phrase "bears all things" translates as "to roof over or to cover with silence." To cover with silence in an interesting translation. Bearing all things requires a level of maturity that includes knowing when to keep our mouths closed and when to just be quiet. Can I bear all things in a quiet manner that will prove to protect our love relationship? The Amplified Bible uses the words, "love bears up under anything and everything that comes." These are powerful words.

Number 11: Love always trusts, or as the AMP puts it; love "is ever ready to believe the best in every person."

Number 12: Love always hopes. "Its hopes are fadeless **under all circumstances.**" (AMP)

Number 13: Love always perseveres. The KJV uses the words "endureth **all things**," and the AMP says that "Love endures everything [**without weakening**]." (emphasis is author's)

"Endureth" translates as "to stay under, remain, undergo, bear trials, have fortitude, abide, tarry and to be patient.

And finally...

Number 14: Love never fails.

The word "fails" in this scripture is the Greek word ekpipto and it translates as "to become inefficient, takes no effect, fades out, to drop away, or to be driven off one's course."

Love refuses to be driven off course.

As we commit to building a strong, solid, and lasting marriage, the Lord will, indeed, direct our hearts and lead us along the path of God's love and Christ's endurance. So, let's lead well, love well, and build according to His blueprint.

PRAYER

Lord, take me by the hand and lead me along the path of God's love and Christ's endurance. May I never stop growing in these areas. I choose today to spend myself in kindness towards my wife. I am determined that I will not be driven off course. I am watching how You love me. I am keeping company with You and learning to live a life of love. I am making my wife my priority and I am ready to demonstrate my total devotion to her as we build our lives together as husband and wife.

HUSBANDS STEP UP YOUR GAME: LEAD. LOVE. BUILD. FIGHT.

BUILD

"Through wisdom a house is built, and by understanding
it is established" – Proverbs 24:3 (NKJV)

HUSBANDS STEP UP YOUR GAME: LEAD. LOVE. BUILD. FIGHT.

DAY 15

I BUILD MY MARRIAGE ON A SURE FOUNDATION

"Through wisdom a house is built, and by understanding it is established" – Proverbs 24:3 (NKJV)

It is time to become wise builders and establish solid and lasting marriages. Let's take a look at Luke 14:28-30 and discover how we can build well.

"For which of you, intending to build a tower, does not sit down first and count the cost, whether he has enough to finish it—lest, after he has laid the foundation, and is not able to finish, all who see it begin to mock him, saying, 'This man began to build and was not able to finish'?" – Luke 14:28-30 (NKJV)

There are two things in this scripture that are of foremost importance.

1. Counting the cost.

2. Laying the right foundation.

Notice that when it comes to building, there is a cost involved. There is an investment to be made and work to be done.

While looking at 1 Corinthians chapter 13, we saw that love and endurance are inseparable. Love is patient. And as men, we know by now, what happens when we attempt to build anything without being patient.

Generally, men like shortcuts. They buy something that has to be put together and they are quick sometimes to toss the instructions aside thinking, "Awe, I don't need these. I can figure this out on my own." Have you ever done that? You didn't want to take the time to first read the directions, so you just laid out all the different parts and pieces and dove in. Three hours later, you had one piece backwards, you stripped at least one screw hole, you chipped a piece of wood off part of the project and you had fourteen extra washers and screws leftover when you were finished (Not to mention that you were in rare form while building and you snapped at everyone who came into the room). If only you had a little bit of patience from the very beginning, not only would you have built that thing in half the time, but you would have built it right.

Patience. Patience is a virtue. Patience is a fruit of the Spirit.
Love is patient.

When my oldest son married, he and his wife moved into a fantastic apartment community in the city where they live. It was their first place together and they were so excited about it. The apartments were fresh and new. They were the very first to live in their unit. The complex was something else. It had walking trails, a saltwater swimming pool with a nice outdoor area fully loaded with grills, and a really hip clubhouse. Every building had its own courtyard area and its own screened in recreational area with table tennis. There was even a place to wash and groom your pets! This place was within walking distance to many wonderful things and it looked perfect, that is, from the outside. Within just a few months, water was leaking from the upstairs unit right into my son's music room, threatening to destroy his instruments and equipment that he had invested so much in; the same equipment that he used to make his living. A lot of his own money and years of his life were invested in that equipment. His dream could have been compromised because someone else did not take the time to build right. Soon my son and his wife were having to vacate. Surprisingly, soon everyone in the entire complex was having to vacate. Why? Because the builders threw those buildings up so fast that although the complex looked great on the outside, it was literally falling apart. What a disappointment. Tenants were given less than a month to move out because of unsafe conditions. There were structural cracks and other deficiencies at the property. News hit the local newspapers, reporting that the apartments were found to be structurally unsound, unsafe, and could face the wrecking ball. Lawsuits were pending, while city engineers began meeting to decide if the place should be fixed or demolished. Imagine that. Eventually, another group came in and purchased the property for 5.3 million. Yes, this was a huge revitalization project for an area of their city at one time. New builders began demolishing parts of the campus and repairing other parts. Think of the money the original builders lost by taking shortcuts. What a senseless loss. What an extreme inconvenience and unnecessary struggle residents suffered all because things were not built properly to begin with.

How have we been building, gentlemen?

We must resist the temptation to look for shortcuts when it comes to building a solid and lasting marriage. As good builders, we must put some key things into place. We really cannot build without these vital elements. First, we must make sure that we are building on the right foundation.

In His Sermon on the Mount, Jesus spoke these words:

> "Therefore whoever hears these sayings of Mine, and does them, I will liken him to a wise man who built his house on the rock: and the rain descended, the floods came, and the winds blew and beat on that house; and it did not fall, for it was founded on the rock. "But everyone who hears these sayings of Mine, and does not do them, will be like a foolish man who built his house on the sand: and the rain descended, the floods came, and the winds blew and beat on that house; and it fell. And great was its fall." – Matthew 7: 24-27 (NKJV)

Gentlemen, The Lord God is that Rock! Build on the Rock. He is our sure foundation. He is the architect and He has drawn up the blueprints for us to follow. He even provides us with the materials to build with, but it is up to us to do the building.

Ephesians 2:20 and 1 Peter 2:6 speak of Jesus as the chief foundation stone. He is the cornerstone on which all the building depends. A cornerstone or foundation stone is the first stone set in the construction of a masonry foundation. It is the most important stone because all other stones will be set in reference to this cornerstone. And this cornerstone will determine the position of the entire structure.

We cannot take shortcuts. We have got to take the time and effort to build the right way now and build it on the solid foundation of Jesus Christ. Christ must be at the center of our marriages. We cannot be like the builder who cut corners in order to finish quickly and turn a quick profit. This builder always loses in the end.

> "Therefore this says the Lord God: "Behold, I lay in Zion a
> stone for the foundation, a tried stone, a precious cornerstone,
> a sure foundation; whoever believes will not act hastily."
> – Isaiah 28:16 (NKJV)

I am reminded of the very powerful hymn that we used to sing many years ago that pretty much says it all:

"My Hope is Built on Nothing Less"
by Edward Mote, 1797-1874

1. My hope is built on nothing less
Than Jesus' blood and righteousness;
I dare not trust the sweetest frame,
But wholly lean on Jesus' name.
On Christ, the solid Rock, I stand;
All other ground is sinking sand.

2. When darkness veils His lovely face,
I rest on His unchanging grace;
In every high and stormy gale
My anchor holds within the veil.
On Christ, the solid Rock, I stand;
All other ground is sinking sand.

3. His oath, His covenant, and blood
Support me in the whelming flood;
When every earthly prop gives way,
He then is all my Hope and Stay.
On Christ, the solid Rock, I stand;
All other ground is sinking sand.

4. When He shall come with trumpet sound,
Oh, may I then in Him be found,
Clothed in His righteousness alone,
Faultless to stand before the throne!
On Christ, the solid Rock, I stand;
All other ground is sinking sand.

What foundation have *you* been building on?

We need to consider that building a solid, lasting marriage will cost us something. It takes some work. It takes some effort. We have to be wise builders and build on the right foundation. We cannot figure this thing out as we go along, but we have to pick up the instruction manual, the blueprint, that Christ has given to us. We can't build this thing our own way, in our own wisdom. We must build our lives on the solid Rock of Jesus Christ, relying on Him to reveal His way and His purposes. As men of God, we build our marriages with the plans and building materials that He has given us. The Bible says that He has given us *all things* that pertain to life and godliness. We are without excuse. We can, indeed, build well.

Proverbs 20:4 says that "If you are too lazy to plow - don't expect a harvest." (CEV) Building takes work. Do work. And decide right now that it is going to be worth it. Your investment, your time, your effort, your energy; it will be worth it. It is your labor of love.

PRAYER

Lord, I am ready to build a strong, solid marriage, one that lasts. I am ready to go back to the blueprints. I am ready to pick up Your Word, follow your instructions, listen to your voice and build it right. I will put the necessary work and effort into my marriage. I will build it on the one and only sure foundation, Jesus Christ. I will build a marriage where You, Lord, are the chief cornerstone. My marriage will be able to withstand the storms of life and every wind of adversity. I am willing to sow into my marriage and I will trust You to bring about a good harvest.

DAY 16

I AM A WISE BUILDER

*"According to the grace of God which was given to me, like a wise master builder I laid a foundation, and another is building on it. But **each man must be careful how he builds** on it. For no man can lay a foundation other than the one which is laid, which is Jesus Christ. Now if any man builds on the foundation with gold, silver, precious stones, wood, hay, straw, each man's work will become evident; for the day will show it because it is to be revealed with fire, and the fire itself will test the quality of each man's work."*
– 1 Corinthians 3:10-13 (NASB)

Building on the right foundation is the key. The storms of life will come. The winds of adversity will blow. At times the floods will threaten to overcome us and our marriage relationship. You better believe that we will walk through some fires, but if we have built on the sure foundation of Jesus Christ, we have nothing to fear. We are talking about the *quality* of the marriages that we are building. We need to take care in the way that we build.

The *Word of God* provides the very framework for building a solid marriage. When it comes to building, the frame is the skeleton of a structure. The framework provides necessary support for everything that follows. If the framework is weak and unstable, no amount of the most beautiful finishing touches will be able to hide the flaws. Eventually, the walls will begin to crack, and the floors will begin to sag. These flaws will begin to show up in the building of a house and they will begin to show up in the building of a marriage and family. We must be men of faith and men who know the Word of God. His holy Word is still for today. God's principles work!

Principle number 1:

"Let the marriage be held in honor [esteemed worthy, precious, of great price, and especially dear] in all things."
– Hebrews 13:4a (AMP)

Do you think of your marriage as precious and especially dear?

The reality is that God Himself ordained marriage. It was His idea from the very beginning. Marriage is from Him. It is to be honored before God and before men. Not only is the institution of marriage to be held in honor, but our very own marriage is to be highly esteemed. We are to treat the marriage itself with honor and we are to treat our spouse with honor. We esteem our wives as worthy of honor. We see our wife as so valuable, so precious and so very dear to us.

1 Peter 3:7 says, "Husbands, live with your wives in an understanding way, showing honor to the woman as the weaker vessel, since they are heirs with you of the grace of life, so that your prayers may not be hindered." (ESV)

Husbands, honor your wife. The word "honor" in 1 Peter 3:7 is the word *timē* and it translates as "a valuing by which the price is fixed, an honoring of the price paid."

First, we honor our wives because God honors them. He saw your wife as so very valuable that He was willing to pay the price of His only Son's very life to redeem her. You too are to value and esteem her to the highest degree. And you are to honor your wife as the *weaker vessel*. Recognizing that her frame is more delicate than yours and her very heart is more tender, you are to exercise a special kindness and protection towards her. Notice also that the word vessel is used here. Understand, gentlemen, that your wife is a vessel and instrument of the Lord. Treat her accordingly. She is also God's gift to you as your helper. You are doing this thing called life, together. You are co-heirs of the grace of life!

Honor your marriage and honor your wife. There is a right way to treat that woman and it is important that you do treat her right so that *your prayers will not be hindered* or cut off. (1 Peter 3:7)

Do you ever feel like your prayers are not reaching heaven? You may want to evaluate how you have been treating your wife.

"However, each man among you [without exception] is to love his wife as his very own self [with behavior worthy of respect and esteem, always seeking the best for her with an attitude of lovingkindness]" – Ephesians 5:33a (AMP)

Has your behavior towards your wife been behavior worthy of respect and esteem? Has your attitude towards her been an attitude of lovingkindness? I'm not sure what storms your marriage has already come through or may be going through right now, but I do know that the Word of God tells us to love our wives in this way without exception.

Colossians 3:19 says, "Husbands, love your wives, and do not be harsh with them." (ESV)

Are you harsh with your wife? The Jamieson, Fausset, and Brown commentary has only one thing to say about this scripture and here it is: "Many who are polite abroad, are rude and bitter at home because they are not afraid to be so there."

Ouch!

This is probably not the best way to build a solid, lasting, and loving marriage, huh? Your attitude towards your marriage and your wife is pretty important. It is so important to God that failure to honor your wife can actually hinder your prayers from reaching His ears.

Let's build according to God's principles in order that we might experience and enjoy thriving marriages, as well as an open heaven above us.

Principle number 2:

> "Christ's love makes the church whole. His words evoke her beauty. Everything he does and says is designed to bring the best out of her." – Ephesians 5:26 (MSG)

As we are striving to love our wives as Christ loves the church, we will do well to remember that even Christ demonstrates His love for His bride through His words.

We are to honor our wives in heart, in action, and in words. We honor her, we appreciate her, and we express it. One of the ways that we demonstrate honor and respect toward our wife is by the way that we speak to her. Our words have power. They have the power to build up or tear down, to wound or to heal, to burden or to refresh.

As we are building great marriages, we need to remember that communication is one of the most important building blocks. Good communication is important to a happy, healthy marriage. Men, we really need to learn how to be good communicators.

Are you a good communicator?

I haven't always had a way with words. Sometimes I open my mouth, and things come out all wrong. I remember one of mine and Jennifer's first official dates. We were at a nice restaurant having a wonderful dinner and I reached across the table, took her hand in mine, looked into her eyes and said these words; "Your face looks clear tonight." … What I was really thinking about was how beautiful she looked, but I didn't choose the right words to express that. What actually came out of my mouth could have been interpreted a few different ways. Much later she laughed about that comment and told me she began wondering if her face had been bumpy and covered in pimples the last time I had seen her. She smiled at me, thinking that it was most likely a compliment, but in the back of her mind, she was wondering! Thank the Lord she agreed to a second date.

The art of communication isn't always something that men are naturally good at. However, it is an area that we most definitely need to work on. The Bible tells us that "Death and life are in the power of the tongue, and they that love it shall eat the fruit thereof." – Proverbs 18:21 (KJV)

Think about that for a moment. What kind of fruit have your words been producing? Have you been satisfied with the consequences of your words?

James 1:19 tells us to be slow to speak. These are wise instructions. It is a good idea to think first before we open our mouths, fellas. I don't want to wound Jennifer's heart with my words. And I am sure that you do not want to wound your wife's heart with yours. We must realize that women are emotional creatures. We cannot talk to our wives any way we want to. They are sensitive and tender-hearted, and God created them that way on purpose and by design. Most likely, your wife is not able to let words roll right off her back in the same way that you or I might be able to. She cannot just turn her emotions on and off anytime she wants to like a light switch. She cannot just "get over it" in a few seconds, the way that you sometimes expect her to. Your words can wound her spirit. Do not be harsh. As James 1:9 suggests, be slow to open that mouth of yours. Take care in how you communicate. Be the man who protects her heart, rather than the man who wounds her heart.

Colossians 4:6 says to "Let your speech always be with grace, seasoned with salt, that you may know how you ought to answer each other." (NKJV)

The Message Bible puts it like this, "Be gracious in your speech. The goal is to bring out the best in others in a conversation, not put them down, not cut them out."

Use your words to honor your wife. Ephesians 4:29 tells us to edify others with our speech that it might *benefit* the hearer. Are your words edifying? Does she benefit from the way that you speak to her?

The KJV uses the word *minister*. "Let no corrupt communication proceed out of your mouth, but that which is good to the use of edifying, that it may **minister** grace unto the hearers."

Have you considered that the words of your mouth can minister to your wife?

The AMP version says that we should be careful how we speak and that we should use our words in a way that will "be a blessing to those who hear." The Message puts it like this; "Watch the way you talk. Let nothing foul or dirty come out of your mouth. Say only what helps, **each word is a gift**." (emphasis is the author's)

Your words are to be **a blessing** and a gift. Your words can minister to her very heart and spirit. Take care in the way that you build, men of God. Honor your wife and honor your marriage.

PRAYER

Lord, thank You for providing the building materials that I need to build this marriage relationship well. I will take care in the way that I build. My wife is precious and dear to me. I truly value her. I will honor her and respect her in my actions and even in my words. I do not want to be harsh or rude. Forgive me, Lord, for the times that I have been careless in this area. I do not want to be the very one who wounds her heart, but instead, I want to be the man who protects her heart and that is what I should be. God forbid that I make her heart miserable in the way that I treat her. I desire to be a gift and a blessing to my wife. She is the love of my life! So, let the words of my mouth edify her, build her up, heal, refresh and actually minister to her. Help me to be a wise builder and let nothing hinder my prayers.

DAY 17

I AM A GOOD COMMUNICATOR

"Let the words of my mouth and the meditation of my heart be acceptable in your sight, O Lord, my rock and my redeemer."
– Psalm 19:14 (ESV)

Communication in a marriage relationship is so important and although we may be good communicators on our jobs or in our own specific area of expertise, we often struggle in finding the right words to communicate how we feel. As a preacher and teacher of the Word of God, I know how to communicate the gospel message in an effective way. However, when relating to my wife, or even my children for that matter, finding the right words to express how I really feel or what I'm really thinking doesn't always come naturally. There might be a number of reasons why many men find this to be true about themselves, but for the sake of this study, we will not explore those reasons. Instead, we will explore what steps we can take to improve and strengthen our communication. It is said that if you will improve your communication, you will improve your overall marriage. So, what do you say, gentlemen? Is there some improvement that needs to be made?

Communication

Communication is a tool that God has given us to knit our hearts and minds together. It creates intimacy. Now, when we think of the word intimacy, we think about sexual intimacy, but sex is not intimacy. It is an expression of intimacy. Intimacy is not about sharing our bodies with one another. Intimacy is the sharing of our hearts with one another. It includes laughing together, crying together and really communicating with one another. And this kind of connectedness leads to and deepens all other forms of intimacy.

The truth is that our communication, as well as our lack of communication, impacts our marriages. Communication is so very important in a marriage relationship, yet studies show that couples spend less than 4 minutes a day in meaningful conversation.

We all have a need for connecting with one another and the primary way that we do that is through meaningful conversation. If a husband and wife feel like they are drifting away from one another, it could be that they have actually "drifted away" from meaningful conversation. They have stopped communicating. They no longer share their hearts with one another. Certainly, it may seem harder to find time to do that as our lives progress and get busier and busier. Regardless, we cannot take our marriage relationship for granted and neglect communication.

Before you were married, you most likely spent hours upon hours, talking about everything under the sun together and enjoying one another's company. After marriage, of course, life gets busier. Children come into our lives and can be quite demanding. While we are raising our children, it may seem impossible at times to have an uninterrupted conversation, let alone any type of deep meaningful conversation.

Many times, our schedules are pretty locked up with our jobs, responsibilities and other commitments. There doesn't seem to be enough hours in one day to accomplish everything that we need to accomplish as it is. Everything else and everyone else is competing for our time and attention from day to day. And it is true that men tend to want nothing more than to unwind after a long day. Possibly they will do that in front of the television or in some other way to tune everything and everyone out for just a little while. After all, we all need a little downtime, right? We need to decompress. We may have a man cave or even a hobby that is our "go to" when we need to shut down our minds and really relax. That's okay, as long as it doesn't lead to a communication breakdown in your marriage. It's okay, as long as you don't get so preoccupied with other things that you no longer make time for her. You see, our wives long for that time of sharing hearts and connecting in this way. A wise builder of his marriage does not neglect these moments that bind hearts together and keep them bound tightly.

You see, we make time for the things that we really do value. If today, your wife began to evaluate how much you love and value her by the amount of time you devote to her, what might she assume? How might she interpret the way that you spend your free time?

Be intentional.

We have to get intentional about spending time together connecting. We may even need to schedule that time. And once we set that time aside for one another, we must be careful to not allow anything to interfere with it. Guard your time with one another.

Be purposeful about setting specific time aside for connecting with your wife. Make it happen.

Sometimes there are plenty of opportunities to do that right there in your home. Other times it might mean getting out of the house. For some, it may mean getting that babysitter on a regular basis to really have some good one on one time together. Go out on a date!

When our children were young, we made excuses for why we couldn't go out on dates. I wanted to whisk Jennifer away for a weekend alone from time to time, but that didn't happen frequently enough. And going out for a nice romantic dinner date...let's face it, most couples raising a family are on a tight budget and may not be able to afford both a fancy dinner out on the town and a babysitter. It took us a while, but we finally realized that we were thinking all wrong about dates. We began to do simple things like going to a local park and enjoying the scenery together. We held hands. She loves to take photographs of all things related to nature. And as I watch her do the things she loves to do, it makes my heart pound. Do you ever stop everything you are doing and just look at your wife? Other times, we would take a drive, park the car downtown and just walk and talk. Often, we would grab a simple cup of coffee together. We could always afford that! It was really about making one another a priority, giving each other time and attention.

Does your wife know that she is your priority?

Still today, we look forward to our coffee dates. Simple is what works best for us. We run off and grab some coffee together at a local coffee shop. We put our phones away. We sit across the table from one another. We look at each other as we talk. And we give one another our undivided attention.

For you, it may be different. It may be a morning breakfast together, or it may be a walk in your own neighborhood after dinner. Whatever works for you. Make it happen, gentlemen. Give your spouse your full, undivided attention. Put away the things that are distracting you. Look at her when she is talking to you and really listen.

Listening is an important part of communication. James 1:19 tells us to be "quick to listen," and slow to speak. The AMPC uses the words "a ready listener". I don't know about you, but I want to be a ready listener. My wife is the most important person in my life. I trust that your wife is the most important person in yours too. When we are only half-listening, it conveys a different message though. It gives her the impression that someone or something is more important to you. So, turn off whatever is distracting you and give her your attention. Remember; whatever is causing you to tune out your spouse is killing your communication and it is killing your intimacy.

When you give her your full attention it says, "You are important to me. How you feel is important to me. What you think is important to me. You matter to me. I value you."

Set aside regular time for your wife. Give her your time and attention. Become a better communicator. Listen to her as she shares her heart and learn to share yours with her.

There may not always be something deep and meaningful to talk about, but make sure your communication extends beyond a four-minute rundown of the events of the day. Make sure that every conversation that you have with your spouse isn't about the bills or some present issue or problem. Enjoy one another's company.

Open up and share your heart. This *opening up* binds us together. It is emotional intimacy and it brings about a healthy relationship.

PRAYER

Lord, I completely understand how important communication is in a marriage relationship. Help me to become a better communicator. Teach me to open up and share my heart with my wife. Make me a ready listener as my wife shares her heart with me. Remind me and nudge me when I am becoming preoccupied with something that is taking precious time and attention away from my wife, especially when she needs me the most. Show me how to demonstrate to her that she matters to me. I will guard my time with my wife as I build my marriage. I will become more intentional in all of these things. Lord, bring about a greater connectedness in my marriage and strengthen this emotional intimacy that our total marriage might grow and thrive.

HUSBANDS STEP UP YOUR GAME: LEAD. LOVE. BUILD. FIGHT.

DAY 18

I HANDLE CONFLICT CORRECTLY

"Like apples of gold in settings of silver is a word spoken in right circumstances." – Proverbs 25:11 (NASB)

In a marriage relationship, communication is so important. It connects our hearts and bonds us together as one. Miscommunication, on the other hand, leads to unnecessary conflict. Conflict serves to divide a husband and wife. The Bible tells us that a house divided against itself cannot stand (Mark 3:25). Therefore, we had better learn how to communicate correctly during times of conflict and disagreement.

Conflict is inevitable, and disagreements will happen, but knowing how to handle them correctly makes all the difference in the world. The Word of God really does give us the instructions and tools to get this thing right, if we are willing…

The Cause of Conflict

"What causes fights and quarrels among you? Don't they come from your desires that battle within you?" – James 4:1 (NIV)

James poses a great question and delivers an honest answer. Taking an honest look at our own heart is always the right place to start. As my wife counsels and ministers to many wives, she finds that women tend to have a hard time seeing just how they themselves are contributing to the issues within their marriages that are causing them to feel so miserable. As I counsel and work with husbands, I find that men often know exactly what they are doing wrong. They clearly see where they are missing it and where they themselves are failing. However, a certain pride and stubbornness within them cause them to refuse to confront and deal with their own personal issues. And it's these issues that are leading to the destruction of their own marriages. Yet, if you ask men if they have a problem with pride, most will tell you they do not.

Questions to ponder:

Am I stubborn?

Do I insist on being right about everything?

Do I stand my ground even when I know that I am not right?

Do I automatically go into self-defense mode when challenged?

Am I short tempered?

Do I struggle with anger?

Verse 6 of James chapter four goes on to say that God resists the proud but gives grace to the humble.

I don't know about you, but I need His grace every single day of my life!

Many times, conflict begins with our own selfishness. The way that we communicate during times of conflict comes straight out of our own stubbornness and pride. We may even react in anger, rather than respond the way the Lord would have us respond. Our own behavior can be damaging to the marriage relationship.

One thing is for sure. We cannot ignore our own heart condition and think for one minute that we are going to build solid, loving marriages that are growing and thriving. That would be much like a builder who finds that he has a piece of untreated lumber that is warped, but instead of going back to the lumber store to get a new piece, he continues to build with the warped board. He knows it's warped but he continues building with it anyway. As he builds, the angles of the rest of the structure are not going to be squared. He continues building, knowing the structure is going to be off center. It's just not going to be right with this piece of twisted wood. And this one warped board is the only thing preventing this structure from being really great.

In essence, isn't that what we are doing when we refuse to deal with our own issues? We must submit these areas of our own heart to the Lord and allow Him to do a work within us. The Lord will make us like new if we will yield to Him. And as we are growing individually, our marriages will be strengthened as well. So, let's acknowledge and own up to our part of this thing. Let's humble ourselves, receive His grace and correction in our lives, and build something great!

Lord, put Your finger on anything in my heart that needs changing and I will submit that area to You.

Reacting versus Responding

Learning how to communicate can save us a lot of trouble. That's what the Word of God says!

> "He who guards his mouth and his tongue keeps himself from troubles." – Proverbs 21:23 (AMPC)

Proverbs 29:20 offers some additional truth we can take to heart: "Do you see a [conceited] man who speaks quickly [offering his opinions or answering without thinking]? There is more hope for a [thickheaded] fool than for him." (AMP)

Yes. I admit it. There have been times that I have answered without thinking. I have reacted with a sharp tongue. Anyone else? Our mere stubbornness can often be at the root of avoidable conflict in our homes. Selfishness, stubbornness, wanting everything our way, being ornery and hard to deal with, being easily angered and spouting off at the mouth; what should we say about this type of behavior? We cannot continue building this way.

We need to take an honest look at how we are accustomed to handling pressure. Do we allow things to build up like a pressure cooker, and then explode? When a conflict arises between ourselves and our spouse, do we react out of our emotions?

> "My dear brothers and sisters, take note of this: Everyone should be quick to listen, slow to speak and slow to become angry, because human anger does not produce the righteousness that God desires." – James 1:19-20 (NIV)

> "He who is slow to anger has great understanding [and profits from his self-control], but he who is quick-tempered exposes and exalts his foolishness [for all to see]." – Proverbs 14:29 (AMP)

The Message Bible puts it like this: "Slowness to anger makes for deep understanding; a quick-tempered person stockpiles stupidity."

Foolishness and stupidity, that is how this kind of behavior is described, straight from the Word of God.

When it comes right down to it, a quick-temper is a heart issue. Reacting out of anger is quite destructive. Words spoken in anger can wound your wife's heart and spirit. Enough words spoken in anger can eventually cause her heart to become numb.

James 3:5-6 reminds us that "It only takes a spark, remember, to set off a forest fire. A careless or wrongly placed word out of your mouth can do that. By our speech we can ruin the world, turn harmony to chaos, throw mud on a reputation, send the whole world up in smoke and go up in smoke with it, smoke right from the pit of hell." (MSG)

When a conflict arises in my marriage relationship, do I react in anger? Am I careless with my words?

The Word of God teaches us that we should actually avoid arguments and conflicts altogether. In fact, the mark of a good leader with good character is to *avoid* quarrels.

"It's a mark of good character to avert quarrels, but fools love to pick fights." – Proverbs 20:3 (MSG)

"It is an honor for a man to keep away from strife [by handling situations with thoughtful foresight], but any fool will [start a] quarrel [without regard for the consequences]." – Proverbs 20:3 (AMP)

Handling Situations with Thoughtful Foresight

So, how do we avoid or even diffuse conflicts?

"Never return evil for evil or insult for insult (scolding, tongue-lashing, berating), but on the contrary blessing [praying for their welfare, happiness, and protection, and truly pitying and loving them]. For know that to this you have been called, that you may yourselves inherit a blessing [from God — that you may obtain a blessing as heirs, bringing welfare and happiness and protection]." – 1 Peter 3:9 (AMPC)

In the midst of a conflict, couples often are quick to hurl insults and sarcastic remarks back and forth at one another. At all costs, avoid these quick comebacks, jabs, and insults. Do not strike back with your words. Stay away from blaming one another or placing guilt on one another. This is not the time for criticism or faultfinding. Instead, do the opposite. Take the opportunity to use your words to redirect the explosive emotions related to the disagreement.

Notice that I said, "Use your words". It is important that you do not think that clamming up and giving your wife the silent treatment is the answer here. Closing your mouth and going to the opposite side of the house is not what is meant by "avoiding" a quarrel. Ignoring a problem in hopes that it will go away all by itself, simply doesn't work. And cutting off the conversation and going to the opposite side of the house creates feelings of rejection. Don't shut down communication. Redirect communication. Here's how:

Proverbs 15:1 says, "A soft and gentle and thoughtful answer turns away wrath, but harsh and painful and careless words stir up anger." (AMP)

Even if she is the one who is picking the fight or creating the conflict, respond the right way. A harsh response is counterproductive. Mean words hurt and they leave your wife's heart in a vulnerable condition. Your response is key. You have the power to decide whether or not an argument actually takes place by how you respond. A gentle response diffuses anger. A soft answer puts out a fire.

Proverbs 16:24 says that "Pleasant words are like a honeycomb, sweetness to the soul and health to the bones."

Pleasant words can bring about healing.

The word "health" in Proverbs 16:24 is the Hebrew word marpe and it translates as "a remedy, a cure, healing, deliverance, and medicine." Many times, the health and strength of your marriage is related to your words.

Now, don't misunderstand me here. I am not talking about becoming a passive "Yes, Dear. No, Dear. Anything you say, Dear" weakling. Quite the opposite. You see, a real man isn't a bully. A real man doesn't treat a woman harshly, cut her down with his words, oppress her, control her or manipulate her. He doesn't make threats or use abusive speech. A real man doesn't blame shift or make excuses. It takes way more strength to back down from an argument, exercise self-control, use wisdom, repair, and even bring about healing.

> "Heaviness in the heart of man maketh it stoop: but a good word maketh it glad." – Proverbs 12:25 (KJV)

Anyone can argue and debate, but a stronger person chooses not to. I have always been a good debater. I enjoy a good debate. I also tend to be competitive. If I am playing a competitive sport or game, I get charged up! This may describe your nature as well. You love to win a debate or even a competitive sport or game. You love winning and hate losing. There isn't necessarily anything wrong with that. However, when it comes to a disagreement or an argument in your marriage relationship, you cannot have this same kind of winner/loser mentality. There is no such thing as a winner or a loser under these circumstances. Because you and your wife are one, you are either winning together or losing together.

Gentlemen, it's time that you win together. Don't waste another day in petty arguments that could be dissolved with a few kind words, a humble spirit, and the Lord's intervention in your situation. Use the power of your words for good and not for evil. Death and life are truly in the power of your tongue. Choose life.

PRAYER

Lord, I pray for continued growth in the area of communication. I realize that my words have the potential to not only wound but stir up anger, create a heaviness and even leave my wife's heart numb towards me. The last thing I want is to leave her heart in a vulnerable condition as she goes out into the world every day facing challenges, battles, warfare, and even temptation. Help me to crucify selfishness and pride in my own life. I don't want to be that person who refuses to deal with their own heart issues. Give me a heart that is quick to repent and yield to Your correction that I might grow in my character, becoming more like You, Jesus. Teach me how to handle conflict correctly and with thoughtful foresight. Teach me how to handle disagreements in a way that will not damage my relationship with my wife, but only stretch it in a way that causes it to grow. Show me how I can respond rather than react. Let all of my words be used to build nothing but a loving and healthy marriage.

"A man takes joy in giving a fitting reply, and how good is a timely word!" – Proverbs 15:23 (BSB)

HUSBANDS STEP UP YOUR GAME: LEAD. LOVE. BUILD. FIGHT.

DAY 19

I AM A MAN WHO WALKS IN FORGIVENESS

"The Lord God hath given me a tongue of the learned, that I should know how to speak a word in season to him that is weary; he wakeneth me morning by morning, he wakeneth mine ear to hear as the learned."
– Isaiah 50:4 (KJV)

Learning to respond correctly in times of conflict can save us a lot of trouble. Words can hurt, but thanks be to God, we are taking responsibility for our words. Men of great strength and integrity take responsibility. A real man willingly admits wrong, apologizes, and even asks for forgiveness. Six of the most powerful words spoken can be these words right here: "I'm sorry. Will you forgive me?"

Forgiveness

The Word of God tells us that we should not even go to sleep before resolving a conflict. There will certainly be times when we don't see eye to eye. That is alright, but don't go to sleep without expressing that even though you may think or feel differently concerning a particular issue, you still love her and will not allow any differences to come between you. Don't begin a new day without letting your wife know that regardless of any differing opinion about any one thing, you still honor, respect, and value her.

There are times when asking her to forgive you is the most appropriate thing to do, and it can bring healing and restoration with it. There is also a time to extend forgiveness, which disarms the enemy and strengthens the oneness you share in your marriage relationship.

If you are angry or upset, get ahold of yourself. Do not act out of those emotions. Learn to release negative thoughts and feelings quickly for the sake of the ongoing strength and health of your marriage. Learn to let things go.

> "Husbands love your wives and be not bitter against them."
> – Colossians 3:19 (KJV)

Yes, things happen that can cause us the kind of pain that seems insurmountable. It is amazing, however, what we can overcome with the power of Christ living on the inside of us. The secret to overcoming is releasing that thing to the Lord. Let Him have it. Let Him carry it. Let Him heal it and turn it around.

Many things can damage a marriage relationship but holding onto hurt is more damaging than anything else. No matter who or what caused the hurt or offense, a barrier is created by it. Allow the barrier to remain and you give the devil a foothold. Remove the barrier through forgiveness and great healing and growth can take place.

We must learn to release hurt and offense quickly and move forward. We shouldn't even lay down and go to sleep without deciding to let that hurt and anger go.

> "In your anger do not sin: Do not let the sun go down while you are still angry, and do not give the devil a foothold."
> – Ephesians 4:26-27 (NIV)

Unforgiveness gives the enemy a foothold. Always remember that! Don't open the door to the enemy and say, "Come on in." We do just that when we hold something against our spouse. Gentlemen, let that thing go!

Unforgiveness is an avenue that Satan uses to gain entrance and access into a believer's life. It is one of his devices. It's a tactic! Paul said in 2 Corinthians 2:10-11, "For if indeed I have forgiven anything, I have forgiven that one for your sakes in the presence of Christ, lest

Satan should take advantage of us; for we are not ignorant of his devices." (NKJV)

Concerning an individual who sinned in their midst, Paul expressed the need to extend forgiveness to him so that Satan would not be able to take advantage of them. You see, we cannot be ignorant about the tactics the enemy uses to come in, divide and conquer. We have got to be wise builders.

I remember in the early years of our marriage, I became so angry with Jennifer that I refused to look at her or speak to her for two days; not one word. I could have held onto that thing and allowed it to destroy our marriage. I am so glad that I didn't. The third day was Sunday and we woke early and began to get ready for church, just as we always had. I should have known that the Lord was going to make me deal with my heart when I came into the House of God. My heart was hard toward her, but it was still soft toward Him. I left her in my trail as I got out of the car and entered the church that morning. I walked down the long hallway and entered an empty classroom because I really wasn't ready to see anyone or speak to anyone. I was in a state. I sat down on a chair in that empty room. On the chair next to me laid an open Bible. I glanced down at the page before me only to read this passage:

> "If you forgive others for their transgressions, your heavenly Father will also forgive you. But if you do not forgive others, then your Father will not forgive your transgressions."
> – Matthew 6:14-15. (NASB)

Was it a coincidence that the Bible left on that seat was opened to this scripture? I don't think so, for I had just whispered a prayer, "Lord, show me what to do in this situation." – And He did...

The very next words that I spoke to her after a grueling 48 hours of the silent treatment were these: "I forgive you." It was interesting how a greater oneness almost immediately took place. We were both released to love one another better than ever before.

After 30 years of marriage, folks see the strength of our marriage and the love that we have for one another and they ask, "What is your secret?" If there is any other secret to building a great marriage, other than putting Christ at the very center of it, it is this: Do not bail out when the going gets tough. There is an old saying; "If you are going through hell, don't stop there. Keep going!" If you will work through every difference, find a way over every hurdle, press through every rough spot, and walk in forgiveness, your marriage will get stronger and become sweeter and sweeter as the years go by.

Live a lifestyle of forgiveness.

> "Therefore as the elect of God, holy and beloved, put on tender mercies, kindness, humility, meekness, longsuffering; bearing with one another, and forgiving one another, if anyone has a complaint against another; even as Christ forgave you, so you also just do." – Colossians 3:12-13 (NKJV)

The word "forgiving" here in this scripture is the word charizomai and it means "to do a favor, show kindness unconditionally, give freely, and grant forgiveness." This word is from the same root as charis, meaning "grace".

> "Forgiveness is made possible through Christ, who forgave us. It is an act in which one person releases another from an offense, refusing to enact the penalty due him or her, refusing to sustain consideration of the cause of the offense, and refusing to allow that offense to affect the relationship. Such forgiveness releases one from a sense of unresolved guilt, restores a clear conscience, and restores relationship. To forgive is not to condone the sin as acceptable, to say it made no difference, or to license repetition of it. Rather, forgiveness is a choice—a decision made to no longer hold an offense against the other person or group." – Raleigh B. Washington

We must become men who walk in forgiveness. Again, we look most like Christ when we forgive. The Bible tells us that He is slow to anger and abounding in love. The Lord is merciful, compassionate, patient, and always ready to forgive. (Neh. 9:31, Exodus 34:6, Psalm 103:8) He is faithful to forgive us and cleanse us from all unrighteousness. (1 John 1:9) It is Christ's nature to forgive, and the Bible tells us in 2 Peter 1:4 that you and I, as born-again believers, can be partakers in His divine nature.

Search my heart, Lord:

Today, does my wife need to hear these six powerful words from me: "I'm sorry. Will you forgive me?"

Have I been holding something against my wife in my heart? Is there something that the Lord is wanting me to release and let go of?

How will I respond?

PRAYER

Lord, help me walk in a spirit of humility. Cause me to become a man who readily admits my own faults and takes responsibility for my wrongs. Let me be quick to repent and make things right. Give me the ability to let go of hurts and offenses right away. Help me to respond correctly in times of conflict and disagree in a way that still honors my wife. In the midst of conflict and disagreements, show me how I can communicate respect and assure my wife of my constant love for her. Give me the right words to speak in all circumstances. Show me your ways, Lord, teach me Your paths.

"So, chosen by God for this new life of love, dress in the wardrobe God picked out for you: compassion, kindness, humility, quiet strength, discipline. Be even-tempered, content with second place, quick to forgive an offense. Forgive as quickly and completely as the Master forgave you. And regardless of what else you put on, wear love. It's our basic, all-purpose garment. Never be without it."
– Colossians 3:12-14 (MSG)

HUSBANDS STEP UP YOUR GAME: LEAD. LOVE. BUILD. FIGHT.

DAY 20

I GUARD THE UNITY IN MY MARRIAGE

"And if a house is divided against itself, that house cannot stand."
– Mark 3:25 (NKJV)

John Gill says that this word "house" in Mark 3:25 refers to "any family, small or great," and that such a "house" cannot stand because "its contentions and discords will soon bring it down from a comfortable and flourishing situation, to a very distressed one."

1 Peter 5:8 tells us to be sober and vigilant. Be alert. Our adversary, the devil, walks about like a roaring lion, seeking whom he may devour. The enemy hates marriage because of what it represents. He works hard to destroy marriage and the family unit. It's time to recognize just what is really happening when any form of chaos comes into our homes. We need to discern just what the enemy is trying to accomplish. It is his plan to divide and conquer. We must never forget that our struggles are not against flesh and blood but against spiritual forces of darkness. Your wife is not your enemy. Your wife is not your adversary or your opponent. She is on your team! We cannot allow our marriages to be destroyed from the inside out through "contentions and discords". Steer clear of any conflict that serves to unravel your unity. As the leaders of our homes, we must guard that unity at all cost. We are not building this thing alone. We are building together as husband and wife. We are building together as one.

"And the two are united into one.' Since they are no longer two but one." – Mark 10:8 (NLT)

A husband and wife have not only been joined together physically, but they have tied their spirits and souls together as one. I believe that there is no greater oneness on earth than that of a husband and wife. Do we understand the power in that kind of oneness?

Unity and Power

There is power in unity. The account of the Tower of Babel gives us a glimpse into the kind of power that is available to us when we are working together as one. When the people who set out to build that tower were in one accord, the Lord God, Himself, said that nothing would be impossible to them because of their great unity. Nothing would able to stop them.

> "Then they said, "Come, let's build a great city for ourselves with a tower that reaches into the sky. This will make us famous and keep us from being scattered all over the world."

> "But the Lord came down to look at the city and the tower the people were building. "Look!" he said. "The people are united, and they all speak the same language. After this, **nothing they set out to do will be impossible for them**! Come, let's go down and confuse the people with different languages. Then they won't be able to understand each other."

> "In that way, the Lord scattered them all over the world, and they stopped building the city. That is why the city was called Babel, because that is where the Lord confused the people with different languages. In this way he scattered them all over the world." – Genesis 11:4-9 (NLT)

These people were unified in their thinking, in their motives, and in their focus. They were unified in their hearts and in their work. God saw the power of their oneness and He stated that nothing they set out to do would be impossible for them. Unfortunately, their efforts were bent on evil intent, wrong motives, and rebellion, so the Lord had to literally confuse their language in order to stop their building and scatter them all over the world.

Note that when they could no longer communicate with one another, their unity was dissolved. Their work was hindered and came to an end. This speaks to me about the importance of communication even in a marriage. If we will get on the same page, set our hearts and focus in the same direction, great strength will be put into place. If we will begin to move in cadence with one another and work together toward the same goals, that unity will take us places. If we will begin to speak the same language and build together as one, nothing will be impossible for us. We will have the life in Christ that He has purposed for us to have. We will know and experience loving, growing, solid, healthy marriages that flourish and no devil in hell will be able to stop it.

Unity and Blessings

Unity is the place where God commands the blessing. In Psalm 133:1 we read, "Behold, how good and how pleasant it is for brethren to dwell together in unity! It is like the precious oil upon the head, running down on the beard, the beard of Aaron, running down on the edge of his garments. It is like the dew of Hermon descending upon the mountains of Zion; for there the Lord commanded the blessing — life forevermore." (NKJV)

God *commands* the blessings upon our lives in the place of unity.

Unity and Answered Prayer

"Husbands, likewise, dwell with them with understanding, giving honor to the wife, as to the weaker vessel, and as being heirs together of the grace of life, that your prayers may not be hindered." – 1 Peter 3:7 (NKJV)

We have already looked at this scripture and noted that our prayers can be hindered when we are not honoring our wives. When there are contentions and discord in the house, it prevents free-flowing, unified prayer.

Albert Barnes states that "it is implied that there might be such a way of living as effectually to hinder prayer; that is, to prevent it's being offered aright, and to prevent any answer. This might occur in many ways. If the husband treated the wife unkindly; if he did not show her proper respect and affection; if there were bickerings, and jealousies, and contentions between them, there could be no hope that acceptable prayer would be offered. A spirit of strife; irritability and unevenness of temper; harsh looks and unkind words; a disposition easily to take offense, and an unwillingness to forgive, all these prevent a "return of prayers."

Here is just another strong reason to guard and protect the unity in our marriage. The Bible teaches us that discord hinders prayer, but when we are in one accord, our prayers are answered. There is power in agreement.

In Matthew 18:19-20, Jesus speaks these words, "Again I say to you that if two of you agree on earth concerning anything that they ask, it will be done for them by My Father in heaven. For where two or three are gathered together in My name, I am there in the midst of them." (NKJV)

What powerful scripture promises. There is a release of power from agreement between any two people. Imagine the power, then, released when a husband and wife pray together from the position of their unique oneness. Imagine the power released when a husband and wife who have joined themselves together in spirit, soul, and body, pray in one accord. There is power in that prayer to reach heaven and a promise to go with it: it will be done for you!

Don't you think that the enemy knows this? He would like nothing more than for you to avoid praying with your wife. Do you suppose that is why at times it is so hard to take the initiative to do just that? Agreement, unity, harmony, being in one accord, all make a profound impact when it comes to many things, including prayer.

Unity and His Presence

The second promise we see in Matthew 18:19 is the promise of His presence. He promised that He would be there in our midst. That's great news because when you have His presence, everything else that you need will be present as well.

Power, blessing, answered prayer, and the presence of God, now that is how we want to build a marriage. Unity is key. Guard that unity and build together as one.

Is there anything dividing myself and my wife right now?

What can I do to remove any barrier?

How can I protect the unity of my marriage relationship?

PRAYER

Lord, reveal to me any area where the enemy has gained access in my marriage. Help me to recognize spiritual attacks and spiritual warfare waged against my marriage. My wife and I are one. My wife is my partner and as we build our lives together, Lord, let nothing hinder our work, our mission or our prayers. Unify us in our hearts, Lord. Unify us in our thinking, our motives, and our focus. Cause us to move forward together in cadence. And continue to teach us about the kind of power we have as a husband and wife in unity.

"Two are better than one, because they have a good reward for their labor." – Ecclesiastes 4:9 (NKJV)

HUSBANDS STEP UP YOUR GAME: LEAD. LOVE. BUILD. FIGHT.

DAY 21

I DEDICATE ALL THAT I AM BUILDING TO THE LORD

"Again I say to you that if two of you agree on earth concerning anything that they ask, it will be done for them by My Father in heaven. For where two or three are gathered together in My name, I am there in the midst of them." – Matthew 18:19-20 (NKJV)

God's Presence in our Midst

"There is a simple and easy way of being happy in the family relation. It is to allow the spirit of Christ and his gospel to reign there." – Albert Barnes

Prayer, worship, and God's presence in our marriages and homes make all the difference in the world. They should not be practiced and experienced in the House of God alone, but in our own house as well. When the apostle Peter spoke of the manner in which the husband was to dwell with his wife in 1 Peter 3:7, he seemed to believe that these things would naturally be taking place but could be *hindered* under certain circumstances.

Albert Barnes states that "it is plainly supposed that united prayer would be one thing that would characterize their living together. He does not direct that there should be prayer. He seems to take it for granted that there would be; and it may be remarked, that where there is true religion in right exercise, there is prayer as a matter of course. The head of a family does not ask whether he must establish family worship; he does it as one of the spontaneous fruits of religion—as a thing concerning which no formal command is necessary. Prayer in the family, as everywhere else, is a privilege; and the true question to be asked on the subject is not whether a man must, but whether he may pray."

Are you exercising your privilege to pray together with your wife on a regular basis?

Is the Lord right in the midst of your marriage relationship?

Is your home a place where the Holy Spirit of God is welcome and dwells?

King Solomon had the ark of the covenant brought in from the city of David after the temple was built. The ark was the symbol of God's manifested presence. Solomon invited in the presence of God, prayed, and dedicated all that he had built to the Lord.

> "I have surely built You an exalted house, and a place for You to dwell in forever." – 1 Kings 8:13 (NKJV)

Go back and read His prayer in 1 Kings chapter eight when you get a chance and you will find that his prayer included these things:

1. Praise and worship. He offered up his praise and his worship to the one true King.

2. Humility. He humbled himself and acknowledged his own unworthiness to be in the presence of an Almighty God.

3. Repentance. He repented and asked for forgiveness for all of Israel's sins, including his own.

4. A prayer for mercy. He asked the Lord to be merciful toward himself and all of the people.

5. A prayer for victory. He asked the Lord to give them victory in every battle.

6. A prayer of restoration. Solomon asked God for His grace to be extended to every area where they had failed in the past, present, and future. He asked God to restore every one of those areas, as only God could do.

This might just be a very good pattern for us to follow as wise builders invoking the hand of God upon our lives, our marriages, our families and our homes.

The ark of the covenant carried the presence of the Lord. It was where His presence remained. It was over the ark that the very glory of God hovered. The ark of the covenant had quite a history, but I would like to bring one other specific account to our remembrance today.

David called for the ark to be brought to Jerusalem and as it was in the process of being transported, the ark began to tip as the oxen stumbled. A man by the name of Uzzah reached out to steady the ark and was struck dead because of the way he handled the presence of God. David was so shaken up by what happened, he was not willing to move the ark any further. Instead, he took it aside into the house of a man named Obed-Edom the Gittite. This man had a heart for God and was ready to house the presence of God.

> "And David was unwilling to move the ark of the Lord into the city of David with him; but David took it aside to the house of Obed-edom the Gittite. Thus the ark of the Lord remained in the house of Obed-edom the Gittite three months, and the Lord blessed Obed-edom and all his household." – 2 Samuel 6:10-11 (NASB)

The Bible tells us that as long as the presence of God was in Obed-edom's home, the blessings of God were upon him and his whole household. During these months, this man and his family were so changed and impacted by the presence of God that Obed-edom never wanted to be without God's presence. When David finally moved the ark to Jerusalem, Obed-edom, along with his entire household went with it. He became a gatekeeper in the tent that housed it (1 Chronicles 26:1-4).

Today, God's presence is no longer limited to an ark in a Holy of Holies. In fact, the Bible teaches us that the believer is now the temple of the Holy Spirit. He resides on the inside of our hearts and we can certainly invite Him to fill our marriages, homes, and families with His presence. Trust me when I say that when we live a lifestyle of prayer and worship in our homes together as man and wife, His presence will be felt there. I remember years ago, my in-laws flew in and spent ten days with us. Ten days is a long time to have guests, by the way. As they left our home, they couldn't stop remarking about how much peace they felt the entire time they were there. They kept trying to describe it.

There is nothing like the presence of God. When we have His presence, we have everything else we need. In His presence, we find freedom, healing, deliverance, provision, safety, protection, blessing, and rest. In His presence, we find peace and fullness of joy. Within His presence, there is comfort, counsel, strength, power, and victory. The Bible says that He is an ever-present help in time of need, and as we are building our marriages we mustn't forget that we need Him!

> "Live in me. Make your home in me just as I do in you. In the same way that a branch can't bear grapes by itself but only by being joined to the vine, you can't bear fruit unless you are joined with me." – John 15:4 (MSG)

Build every part of your life with Christ at the center of it. Abide in Him and He will dwell with you. His presence will be with you, causing you to bear fruit. The Word of God says that apart from Him we can do nothing. The more we walk with Jesus, the more we know this to be true. God is our true source. We sure don't want to do this thing called marriage without Him.

In this unit, we have likened the building of a marriage to the building of a physical structure like a home. If we want to build it to last, we understand that we can't cut corners or take any shortcuts. We know there is a cost and we are willing to pay it. We build it on the right foundation which is Christ. We are careful with the way that we build so we build the very framework with the Word of God. His Word is still for today. His precepts, principles, and instructions still work!

Before a builder begins to put up walls in the structure, he installs a protective barrier known as a house wrap. This house wrap prevents the structure from getting wet and ultimately molding or rotting. It ensures that all the damaging moisture remains on the outside. Unity in the marriage is like that house wrap. Nothing destructive can penetrate it. Insulation is another component and one a builder would never dream of leaving out. The insulation is installed in the floors, in the walls, and in the ceiling. How well a house is insulated is a critical factor when it comes to the home's energy and efficiency. Prayer is that insulation. And, of course, a structure is not very functional without the plumbing and mechanical components from the ductwork, the venting, water heaters, right down to the wiring. The presence and power of God moving and working in our midst makes all the difference in the world. So, men of God, guard your unity at all cost. Pray together on a regular basis. As you are building together as one, dedicate your marriage and home to the Lord and invite Him in. Ask Him to fill your relationship and your home with His presence.

The Bible tells us that two are certainly better than one, but a three-stranded cord is not easily broken. When God is present in our union, we see this illustration of a three-stranded cord mentioned in Ecclesiastes 4:12 come to light. Two strands twisted together are stronger than one alone, as long as they do not become untwisted or unraveled. In that case, they could easily break. God is the third cord and we must be joined to Him. What is interesting in the natural is that a three-stranded rope or cord is actually the strongest kind. One might think that by adding even more strands the cord would become stronger and stronger, but that is not the case. Three-strands are stronger because every single cord is touching one another; not so when you add more strands. The rope may become thicker, but not necessarily stronger. Three strands are the strongest.

When we are tied together as husband and wife and united with Christ as well, we are a three-stranded cord. Not only will we have greater productivity, bear greater fruit, and have a greater reward, but we will experience greater victory.

In context, Ecclesiastes 4:9-12 speaks of greater victory over our enemies. You can be sure that we will face much resistance from the enemy as we build, but with Christ, we will have the victory.

PRAYER

Lord, I dedicate my marriage to You today. I invite you into my marriage, my home, and my family. Come and fill our lives, Lord, with Your presence and Your power. We need you, Lord. I declare this day that You reign in my life, in my marriage relationship, and in my home. Cause us to bear good fruit as we build. I will build my marriage on the sure foundation of Jesus Christ. I will be a wise builder. I will become a good communicator. I will handle conflict correctly. I will walk in forgiveness and guard the unity in my marriage. Let Your blessings and favor be upon us now as husband and wife. In Jesus' name.

"For God's Word is solid to the core; everything he makes is sound inside and out. He loves it when everything fits, when his world is in plumb-line true. Earth is drenched in God's affectionate satisfaction." – Psalm 33:4-5 (MSG)

FIGHT

"Remember the Lord, great and awesome, and fight for your brethren, your sons, your daughters, your wives, and your houses." – Nehemiah 4:13-14 (NKJV)

HUSBANDS STEP UP YOUR GAME: LEAD. LOVE. BUILD. FIGHT.

DAY 22

I WILL FIGHT FOR MY MARRIAGE

"Keep a cool head. Stay alert. The Devil is poised to pounce and would like nothing better than to catch you napping."
– 1 Peter 5:8 (MSG)

I can't help but think of an image that is stuck in my mind from this past week. My wife and I were driving down the road in the middle of the afternoon and came to a very busy intersection where a good bit of road construction was going on. The workers, however, were all lying down on the grassy area right beside the road napping with their hats pulled over their eyes. There they lay on the ground, all stretched out in a perfect row. I smacked my wife's arm and said, "Look. Look at that! Quick. Take a picture." The traffic light changed, and I had to keep going before she had time to snap a photo. We both chuckled at the sight and then she asked, "Is that safe?"

Whether or not it was safe, I cannot say, but what I do know is that our enemy the devil would like nothing better than to catch us napping on the job. What do I mean by that, you might ask. I mean that the enemy of our soul would like to catch us off guard with our eyes all covered up. He likes to blindside us. He loves to launch his attacks when we don't see them coming.

The enemy wages war against us, but because it is an invisible war, we forget that it exists and that it is real. It cannot be seen with natural eyes and unfortunately, many of us have never developed our spiritual sight. Like those men taking a little afternoon siesta, we have become too relaxed with eyes all covered up in the middle of a danger zone. It's not like we haven't been warned. We have.

The Word of God tells us that we have an enemy and identifies him for us. We are told that our struggles are not against flesh and blood but against powers, principalities, and spiritual forces of darkness. The devil and his cohorts plot against us and are looking for opportunities to attack. We have been instructed and urged to be alert and on guard when it comes to the enemy's schemes, strategies, and assignments against us. The enemy is poised and ready to tear down all that we are building. That is why we need to build with eyes wide open, spiritual eyes, that is.

> "Be alert, be on watch! Your enemy, the Devil, roams around like a roaring lion, looking for someone to devour."
> – 1 Peter 5:8 (GNT)

Be alert. Be on watch!

When we look at the account of the rebuilding of the wall in Jerusalem, we see that the builders almost immediately experienced opposition and resistance as they began to work. The surrounding enemies conspired against them to put a stop to their building. As we read Nehemiah chapter four, we can see the tactics that were used against those people. We can also see what kind of action the people took in response.

> "But it so happened, when Sanballat heard that we were rebuilding the wall, that he was furious and very indignant, and mocked the Jews. And he spoke before his brethren and the army of Samaria, and said, "What are these feeble Jews doing? Will they fortify themselves? Will they offer sacrifices? Will they complete it in a day? Will they revive the stones from the heaps of rubbish—stones that are burned?" Now Tobiah the Ammonite was beside him, and he said, "Whatever they build, if even a fox goes up on it, he will break down their stone wall." – Nehemiah 4:1-3 (NKJV)

The first tactic their adversaries used was criticism and mocking. Their goal was to shake the confidence of the builders and to bring about great discouragement, but Nehemiah came against that discouragement with prayer. It was the kind of prayer that invited God into the situation and stirred their faith until they continued to build with even greater focus and greater strength.

"So we built the wall, and the entire wall was joined together up to half its height, for the people had a mind to work." (Verse 6)

They kept on building and they were making great progress, but the more progress they made, the more their enemies conspired against them.

"Now it happened, when Sanballat, Tobiah, the Arabs, the Ammonites, and the Ashdodites heard that the walls of Jerusalem were being restored and the gaps were beginning to be closed, that they became very angry, and all of them conspired together to come and attack Jerusalem and create confusion." (Verses 7-8)

When the mocking, discouraging, and intimidating didn't stop the builder's work, the new tactic of the enemy was to create confusion. Does this sound familiar? Have the attacks launched against you caused you to feel less than capable, discouraged, and at times utterly confused? If so, pay attention to the response of the people.

"Nevertheless we made our prayer to God, and because of them we set a watch against them day and night." (Verse 9)

If you take some time to read the entire fourth chapter of Nehemiah, you will discover that the plot against them was overheard by a few faithful Jews and they warned the builders that an attack was coming. Upon hearing about the enemies' plan, Nehemiah put two things into action. He prayed, and he set a watch against the enemy day and night. This "watch" was pretty important because the adversaries were planning a surprise attack. They were counting on the builders being completely blindsided.

> "And our adversaries said, "They will neither know nor see anything, till we come into their midst and kill them and cause the work to cease." (Verse 11)

The plan was to catch God's people off guard while they were building, but upon hearing of this plan, Nehemiah organized a defense.

> "Therefore I positioned men behind the lower parts of the wall, at the openings; and I set the people according to their families, with their swords, their spears, and their bows. And I looked, and arose and said to the nobles, to the leaders, and to the rest of the people, "Do not be afraid of them. Remember the Lord, great and awesome, and fight for your brethren, your sons, your daughters, your wives, and your houses." (Verses 13-14)

Those men of God got into position. They remembered the Lord and His might, and they understood that their marriages, families, and homes were worth fighting for! When their enemies heard that the builders were on to their plan and ready to do battle, they shrunk back and retreated.

> "And it happened, when our enemies heard that it was known to us, and that God had brought their plot to nothing, that all of us returned to the wall, everyone to his work." (Verse 15)

The people continued building. And this time as they were building, they worked with their eyes wide open. They were prepared. In fact, they never laid down their weapons. They labored with their building materials in one hand and their weapons in the other. They were ready for any attack of the enemy. They were not going to be blindsided or defeated. They were not going to be caught napping. Instead, they were alert, on watch, and ready to fight.

"So it was, from that time on, that half of my servants worked at construction, while the other half held the spears, the shields, the bows, and wore armor; and the leaders were behind all the house of Judah. Those who built on the wall, and those who carried burdens, loaded themselves so that with one hand they worked at construction, and with the other held a weapon." (Verses 16-17)

PRAYER

Lord, give me spiritual discernment and help me to see with spiritual eyes. Develop me in this area. I know who my real enemy is. Expose the enemy and his assignments over my life and my marriage. I am alert, on watch, and ready to fight. My marriage is worth fighting for. I will not be caught off guard. I will not be blindsided, and I will not be defeated.

DAY 23

I RESIST THE DEVIL AND HE FLEES

"The thief does not come except to steal, and to kill, and to destroy."
– John 10:10a (NKJV)

We know who that thief is, don't we? There is one who comes with the desire to steal from us and rob us from experiencing God's best in our lives. Our enemy is ready to kill the plan and purposes of God in every part of our lives, including our marriages. His plan is to destroy us and everything that we are building. He would like nothing more than to ruin our witness and render our Christian testimony useless. Not only would he like for us to lose our marriages, but also our very own souls. What I am saying is that we have got to get a clue when it comes to the attacks on the Christian Marriage, especially our own marriage. With a staggering 50 percent divorce rate among married couples, unbelievers and believers alike, it is clear that the enemy desires to destroy marriage and the family unit as a whole. That is why we need to build with eyes wide open. It's time for the men of God to be alert, to be on watch and prepared for battle. We cannot be ignorant of the enemy's tactics any longer. We must learn to stand guard, resist, push back, and fight.

Stand Guard

Great ancient cities like Jerusalem had thick walls around the entire city. The watchmen took their place upon the walls and in the towers to look upon the land. The watchmen were guards who were assigned to specific territories. Their main task was to look out for any signs of disturbance or schemes and activity of the enemy. It was their job to report anything suspicious to the commander. If there was any threat at all, the gates were shut. If they saw any sign of an army approaching, they sounded the warning and the people prepared for battle.

When it comes to our marriage, family, and home, we need to be watchmen looking out with spiritual eyes, discerning the enemy's schemes and activity. This is our assigned territory. It is vital that we take our position and exercise our authority over the enemy.

While the wall was being rebuilt in Jerusalem, there were still gaps in the wall that were referred to as "exposed places". The watchman guarded and took extra care to protect those weak or exposed places. During the process of building a strong, healthy marriage, there are areas that we are still working on. These are areas that are currently vulnerable. The enemy is looking for a way that he can get in and wreak havoc. We must take special care to guard the weak places.

In ancient times, watchtowers were placed overlooking the fields. When the crops were ripening, and it was close to the time of harvest it was vital that a watchman was present to guard the field against animals and even thieves. The entire community's food and sustenance were at stake. You have been working and sowing into your marriage and home. Let no enemy come in and steal, kill or destroy what you have been laboring for. That harvest belongs to you.

Resist and Push Back

James 4:7 tells us that if we submit to God and resist the devil, he will flee. Virtually this is what we saw take place in Nehemiah chapter four. When the adversaries realized that God's people were not going to allow them to come right in and destroy them, they retreated. I love how Nehemiah put these enemies in their place in verse twenty of chapter two.

> "But when Sanballat the Horonite, Tobiah the Ammonite official, and Geshem the Arab heard it, they laughed at us

and despised us, and said, "What is this thing that you are doing? Will you rebel against the king?" So, I answered them, and said to them, "The God of heaven Himself will prosper us; therefore we His servants will arise and build, but you have not heritage or right or memorial in Jerusalem."
– Nehemiah 2:18-20 (NKJV)

Technically, Nehemiah's enemies didn't have any right to hinder, attack, stop or destroy, anyone or anything in this situation. And they certainly did not have any heritage or memorial in that place. Nehemiah had actually obtained letters from the king granting them legal protection to go in and build.

"Furthermore I said to the king, "If it pleases the king, let letters be given to me for the governors of the region beyond the River, that they must permit me to pass through till I come to Judah, and a letter to Asaph the keeper of the king's forest, that he must give me timber to make beams for the gates of the citadel which pertains to the temple, for the city wall, and for the house that I will occupy." And the king granted them to me according to the good hand of my God upon me. Then I went to the governors in the region beyond the River, and gave them the king's letters." – Nehemiah 2:7-9 (NKJV)

Well, there you have it. The leaders from the surrounding areas had no business organizing any form of attack whatsoever against God's people. But just like our enemy, the devil, a lot of usurping was going on. The enemy of our soul has no legal right or authority over us, our marriages, our families or anything we are building. He is a poser, a usurper, and a thief. We too have the favor and protection of our King Jesus and the written Word of God. And like Nehemiah, we must answer the enemy's attacks by letting him know that he has no heritage, no right or memorial in any part of our lives. We must remind him that he is a defeated foe. We must put him in his place and continue to move forward in victory. Men of God, it is vital that we take our position and exercise our authority over the enemy.

We must guard that which we are building and learn how to fight our battles. We cannot sit back idly and let the enemy come in and take territory. There are some things that are worth fighting for, and our marriages are one of those things. So, what are you waiting for, men of God? Get dressed for battle!

> 'Finally, my brethren, be strong in the Lord and in the power of His might. Put on the whole armor of God, that you may be able to stand against the wiles of the devil. For we do not wrestle against flesh and blood, but against principalities, against powers, against the rulers of the darkness of this age, against spiritual hosts of wickedness in the heavenly places. Therefore take up the whole armor of God, that you may be able to withstand in the evil day, and having done all, to stand."

> "Stand therefore, having girded your waist with truth, having put on the breastplate of righteousness, and having shod your feet with the preparation of the gospel of peace; above all, taking the shield of faith with which you will be able to quench all the fiery darts of the wicked one. And take the helmet of salvation, and the sword of the Spirit, which is the word of God; praying always with all prayer and supplication in the Spirit, being watchful to this end with all perseverance and supplication for all the saints" — Ephesians 6:10-18 (NKJV)

We have been told point blank that we have an enemy. We have been warned that an attack is coming. We have been advised to be alert and on watch, but that's not all. The Lord has equipped us with armor and He has given us weapons to fight with. It is up to us, however, to do the watching, the dressing, and the fighting.

Will you wake up and suit up? Will you pick up your weapons? Will you fight?

> "Remember the Lord, great and awesome, and fight for your brethren, your sons, your daughters, your wives, and your houses." – Nehemiah 4:13-14 (NKJV)

PRAYER

Lord, my marriage and my home are my assigned territories. I will stand guard. I will resist, and I will push back. I will take my position and exercise my God-given authority. I stand against the wiles of the devil. I will not sit back idly and allow the enemy to destroy my marriage. It is too important to me. I will rise up and build. And I will rise up and fight. Lord, show me just what battles are of utmost importance for me to fight and win today.

DAY 24

I AM WINNING MY OWN PERSONAL BATTLES

"Our tools are ready at hand for clearing the ground of every obstruction and building lives of obedience into maturity."
– 2 Corinthians 10:6 (MSG)

Clearing the Ground of Every Obstruction

We have been equipped with the tools that we need for building as well as the weapons we need for fighting. And both go hand in hand. In Nehemiah chapter four, the builders were trying to get that wall finished before the enemy came to attack, but there was one thing that was seriously obstructing their progress.

> "Then Judah said, "The strength of the laborers is failing, and there is so much rubbish that we are not able to build the wall." – Nehemiah 4:10 (NKJV)

The builders came to a place of great discouragement. They were completely overwhelmed with the "rubbish" or debris that was piled up. The ruins were a hindrance, prolonging the work of the actual building. The burned and broken stones of the previous walls were in a heap all around them. Dirt, dust, dry earth, powder, ashes, mortar, and whatever else existed had to be hauled off. Clearing the area of all the rubbish was no easy task. The strength of the laborers seemed to be giving out. They grew weary and began to complain because of the difficulty. The quantity of the rubbish was so great, and the work just seemed too hard. Nevertheless, it had to be cleared away. It had to be done. It could not be avoided. There was no way they could rebuild on this foundation without first clearing away the rubbish. Otherwise, the wall would not be able to stand. There was no doubt about it. They would have to clear the ground of every obstruction before they could finish their building.

We too must clear the ground of every obstruction. We must deal with our own rubbish. No matter how long and how hard we try to avoid it, no matter how big a task it may seem to be, the truth remains. Our own personal sin issues impede the building of a strong, healthy marriage. And our rubbish leaves us vulnerable to the attacks of the enemy.

The greatest battles that need to be fought and won are our own personal battles. Those things that have become strongholds in our lives need to be confronted. These are the battles that need winning immediately. These are the enemies that we must engage right away. There are some things in our own personal life that need to be defeated, conquered, overthrown and demolished. Men of God, it is time to gain victory over the battles of our own hearts. We cannot ignore them any longer. We cannot sit back idly as if they do not exist. We must rise up like the warriors that we were created to be and conquer them, no matter what it takes.

> "The kingdom of heaven suffers violence and the violent take it by force." – Matthew 11:12 (NKJV)

The idea of taking it by force in Matthew 11:12, is that there are a pressing and a fighting going on. The Pulpit Commentary gives a vivid description of those who engage in this kind of fight:

> "Men whose mind is made up and who care not what force and power they employ to attain the object. Take it by force; "grasp it for themselves," like rough and violent bandits seizing their prey."

Now that is a picture of outright desperation. How desperate are you to be free from the things that have hindered you and held you captive? How bad do you want victory, Man of God? Are you willing to engage in some pressing and fighting for it?

Adam Clarke says, "He that will take; get possession of the kingdom of righteousness, peace, and spiritual joy, must be in earnest; all hell will oppose him every step he takes; and if a man be not absolutely determined to give up his sins and evil companions, and have his soul saved at all hazards, and at every expense, he will perish everlastingly. This requires a violent earnestness."

How about you, Man of God? Are you desperate to be free from every stronghold in your life? Are you determined to do whatever you have to do to gain victory? Is your mind made up that you will fight and win the battles of your own soul? Are you a violent man as described in Matthew 11:12?

"The violent man, determined to take the kingdom by force, goes to war with his sins, makes no excuse for them, never pretends to say they are venial, or to say that they are natural. He must be rid of them, and he knows it, or he cannot enter heaven. Therefore he brings the fire and the sword of the new kingdom into their encampments and into their fastnesses, burns and slays without mercy, as though they were his enemies, counts nothing worth keeping if it involves truce, treaty, or compromise with them." – C.J. Vaughan

Men of God, your personal sin battles that you have not yet gained victory over have become the rubbish that is impeding your progress. It is the very thing that has become the hindrance prolonging the actual building of your marriage. God has given you the tools necessary for clearing the ground of any and every obstruction. What will you do with them?

"For our weapons of warfare are mighty. "For the weapons of our warfare are not physical [weapons of flesh and blood], but they are mighty before God for the overthrow and destruction of strongholds." – 2 Cor 10:4 (AMPC)

Our weapons are mighty before God for overthrowing and destroying strongholds. The question is not "can I destroy them?" The question is "will I destroy them?"

Will you choose to fight?

There was a time when King David decided that he would *not* fight, and that decision opened the door to all kinds of pain, grief, and failure in his life.

> "It happened in the spring of the year, at the time when kings go out to battle, that David sent Joab and his servants with him, and all Israel; and they destroyed the people of Ammon and besieged Rabbah. But David remained at Jerusalem." – 2 Samuel 11:1 (NKJV)

It was a time when kings went to battle, but David stayed in Jerusalem. He refused to go to battle and sent someone else in his place. We are not told why, and it leaves us wondering because it was completely out of character for this man of God. David's legacy and his victories in war are recorded throughout the annals of history. This is the same fearless man who killed the lion and the bear, the same David who took down the giant Goliath with a sling and a stone. He pursued the Amalekites after the destruction of Ziklag and overtook them. We read about him destroying the Philistines in the book of First Samuel, yet this same David refused to even go to battle in the book of Second Samuel. What had changed? Was he tired of fighting? Was he bored with the routine? Was he looking for an escape from reality? Whatever the reason was, it proved to be a bad decision. His failure to go to war and fight lead to his greatest moral failure. We know the story. Instead of going to battle like the other kings, he was up one evening and from his rooftop, he saw a beautiful woman bathing. He lusted after her, had her brought to his home, committed adultery with her and impregnated her. David clearly was in the wrong place at the wrong time. If only he had gone to battle with the other kings…

He refused to go to battle and he refused to take care of his personal issues. He even refused to repent. Instead, he had Bathsheba's husband killed to cover up his sin. It wasn't hidden from God though. God sent the prophet Nathan to speak a word to David to deal with his unrepentant heart. Make no mistake about it. It is always better to bring your failures to God before He brings His judgement to you. In some way, for some reason, and by some set of circumstances, David was unwilling to fight at the time of war.

Men of God, don't make this same mistake. Don't let the enemy take the fight out of you. If you stop fighting, you stop winning. You cannot celebrate a victory without a fight. It is important that you conquer and win your own battles. These victories are not only for you, but they are for your wife, your children, your grandchildren, and for future generations to come.

What battles are you winning so that your bride can walk in victory?

PRAYER

Lord, I realize that I cannot build well with my own rubbish all around me cluttering up the foundation. I am willing to do away with, slay and put my own sin to death. No longer will I stay in a place of denial for that only serves to weaken me. I will not avoid this battle. I will face every one of my own challenges. I will engage the enemy and fight. Help me to overthrow and destroy every stronghold in my life, Lord, that I might walk in freedom and victory.

"So let God work his will in you. Yell a loud no to the Devil and watch him scamper. Say a quiet yes to God and he'll be there in no time. Quit dabbling in sin. Purify your inner life. Quit playing the field. Hit bottom, and cry your eyes out. The fun and games are over. Get serious, really serious. Get down on your knees before the Master; it's the only way you'll get on your feet."
– James 4:7-10 (MSG)

DAY 25

I KEEP MYSELF PURE

"Keep back Your servant also from presumptuous sins; let them not have dominion over me." – Psalm 19:13 (NKJV)

What has you pressed down? What sin has enslaved you? What stronghold have you been dealing with (or refusing to deal with)? For you, it might be anger. It might even be an addiction to something as serious as drugs, alcohol, or pornography. For David it was lust. For many men, it is pride. Whatever it might be, if there is anything at all, it is time to face your giant. It is time to confront your enemies.

As I counsel husbands who are struggling in their marriage relationships, the above strongholds tend to be at the root of many marriage problems. The battle with pornography is becoming increasingly more common. It's a sin issue that is rapidly destroying marriages and I might add, destroying men's lives. And for those reasons, we need to bring attention to it in this chapter.

One of the most common sin issues or strongholds in men's lives today: pornography.

The Family Research Council did a study on the effects of pornography on the family and on the individual. Here are some of the results from their findings:

The Family and Pornography

- Married men who are involved in pornography feel less satisfied with their conjugal relations and less emotionally attached to their wives. Wives notice and are upset by the difference.

- Pornography use is a pathway to infidelity and divorce and is frequently a major factor in these family disasters.

- Among couples affected by one spouse's addiction, two-thirds experience a loss of interest in sexual intercourse.

- Both spouses perceive pornography viewing as tantamount to infidelity.

- Pornography viewing leads to a loss of interest in good family relations.

The Individual and Pornography

- Pornography is addictive, and neuroscientists are beginning to map the biological substrate of this addiction.

- Users tend to become desensitized to the type of pornography they use, become bored with it, and then seek more perverse forms of pornography.

- Men who view pornography regularly have a higher tolerance for abnormal sexuality, including rape, sexual aggression, and sexual promiscuity.

- Prolonged consumption of pornography by men produces stronger notions of women as commodities or as "sex objects."

- Pornography engenders greater sexual permissiveness, which in turn leads to a greater risk of out-of-wedlock births and STDs. These, in turn, lead to still more weaknesses and debilities.

- Child-sex offenders are more likely to view pornography regularly or to be involved in its distribution.

This sin of pornography may be a "hidden sin" in many cases, but it is not hidden from God. Without bringing this area into submission to God, it becomes a stronghold bringing shame and guilt along with it. It alienates us from God. And it will cause a tearing down of the intimacy and trust in a marriage relationship. It is detrimental to the individual. It is detrimental to the spouse. It is detrimental to the family.

Consider the wise words of Solomon from Proverbs chapter 5:

> "Do you know the saying, 'Drink from your own rain barrel, draw water from your own spring-fed well'? It's true. Otherwise, you may one day come home and find your barrel empty and your well polluted. Your spring water is for you and for you only, not to be passed around among strangers. Bless your fresh-flowing fountain! Enjoy the wife you married as a young man! Lovely as an angel, beautiful as a rose—don't ever quit taking delight in her body. Never take her love for granted! Why would you trade enduring intimacies for cheap thrills with a whore? For dalliance with a promiscuous stranger? Mark well that God doesn't miss a move you make; he's aware of every step you take. The shadow of your sin will overtake you; you'll find yourself stumbling all over yourself in the dark. Death is the reward for an undisciplined life; your foolish decisions trap you in a dead end." – Proverbs 5:15-23 (MSG)

Traps and dead ends. The truth from the Word of God is that we can overcome all temptations and sin in our lives.

> "No temptation has overtaken you except such as is common to man; but God is faithful, who will not allow you to be tempted beyond what you are able, but with the temptation will also make the way of escape, that you may be able to bear it." – 1 Corinthians 10:13 (NKJV)

God always gives us a way out. We are not to allow sin to have dominion over us, but we are to rule over it. Christ made provisions on the cross for us to be free from the bondage of sin.

Pornography not only entraps and enslaves men, destroying their lives, but it is a tool in the hands of the enemy to destroy the wife's life too. It dishonors the marriage. It dishonors the wife. And it dishonors God.

God tells us in His Word that "Marriage should be honored by all, and the marriage bed kept pure, for God will judge the adulterer and all the sexually immoral." – Hebrews 13:4 (NIV)

The word "pure" in Hebrews 13:4 means to be undefiled or unsoiled. Men of God, understand that in order for us to keep the marriage bed pure, we are going to have to first keep ourselves pure.

> "Run away from sexual immorality [in any form, whether thought or behavior, whether visual or written]. Every other sin that a man commits is outside the body, but the one who is sexually immoral sins against his own body. Do you not know that your body is a temple of the Holy Spirit who is within you, whom you have [received as a gift] from God, and that you are not your own [property]? You were bought with a price [you were actually purchased with the precious blood of Jesus and made His own]. So then, honor and glorify God with your body." – 1 Corinthians 6:18-20 (AMP)

Honor and glorify God with your body.

We are warned in the Word of God to flee, run away from, have nothing to do with sexual immorality in any form, including thought, behavior, visual, or written. We are to honor and glorify God with our bodies. Are your eyes part of your body? Is your mind part of your body? I'll stop there... Your body is a temple and dwelling place for the Spirit of God. Your body is a sacred place. Your body is not your own.

We cannot separate our sexual lives from the rest of our lives, but it is amazing how many men are willing to submit all other areas of their lives to God but this area. Remember our key scripture just a few chapters back, "Submit yourselves therefore to God. Resist the devil, and he will flee from you." (James 4:7) If there is no submitting of the area to God, there will be no fleeing of the devil. If there is no resisting on our part, there will be no ceasing on the enemy's part.

Submit and resist.

"There is a sense in which sexual sins are different from all others. In sexual sin we violate the sacredness of our own bodies, these bodies that were made for God-given and God-modeled love, for 'becoming one' with another." – 1 Corinthians 6:18 (MSG)

God has given us a gift. Let's protect it!

"God honored the Master's body by raising it from the grave. He'll treat yours with the same resurrection power. Until that time, remember that your bodies are created with the same dignity as the Master's body. You wouldn't take the Master's body off to a whorehouse, would you? I should hope not." (Verses 14-16)

Dignity. Your body was created with dignity; the same dignity as the Master's body. And not just *your* body. Your wife's body has been created with dignity as well. To treat her body with anything less than dignity is to dishonor her. Anytime that you handle her body in a way that is degrading or cheap, you have dishonored her and defiled the marriage bed. If the way that you are treating her body is causing her to feel devalued or to feel shame, you are dishonoring her. Keep your heart pure. Honor God. Honor your marriage. Honor the gift of oneness. Honor your wife. Keep the marriage bed pure and guard the sacredness of sexual intimacy in your marriage.

"There's more to sex than mere skin on skin. Sex is as much spiritual mystery as physical fact. As written in Scripture, "The two become one." Since we want to become spiritually one with the Master, we must not pursue the kind of sex that avoids commitment and intimacy, leaving us more lonely than ever – the kind of sex that can never "become one." (Verses 16-17)

"Sexual drives are strong, but marriage is strong enough to contain them and provide for a balanced and fulfilling sexual life in a world of sexual disorder. The marriage bed must be a place of mutuality—the husband seeking to satisfy his wife, the wife seeking to satisfy her husband. Marriage is not a place to "stand up for your rights." Marriage is a decision to serve the other, whether in bed or out." – 1 Corinthians 7:3-5 (MSG)

Marriage is strong enough to contain your sexual drive. It is the "sexual disorder" in the world around us that the enemy uses to tempt and trap even the married man. There is not a day that goes by that I do not see the news reporting on another man convicted of sexual misconduct of some kind. Whether it is pornography related, sex trafficking or another teacher arrested for engaging in sex with a student, it's on the news every day. Sadly, those whose lives are falling prey are teachers and leaders, reputable businessmen in the community, our neighbors, and even our local clergy. It's disappointing, yet it's everywhere, and as Genesis 4:7 puts it "sin is crouching at your door; it desires to have you, but you must rule over it." Don't open that door. If you have already opened that door, repent and close the door immediately. Then keep it shut. It's part of what we have been talking about; ruling over sin in our own lives, fighting and winning our own personal battles—clearing away the rubbish in our own personal lives, whatever it might be. Let's not wait one more day! Your issues affect way more than little old you. They affect the strength and health of your marriage.

PRAYER

Lord, I declare today that sin will not have dominion over me. I will rule over it. I will walk in the freedom that You have purchased for me. I will keep myself pure. I will honor and glorify you with my body. I will protect the gift of intimacy that you have given to me and my wife. I will honor my wife and I will keep the marriage bed pure. I will lead a disciplined life in Jesus Christ's name. And I will fight and win my own personal battles.

"I will walk about in freedom, for I have sought out your precepts."
– Psalm 119:45 (NIV)

HUSBANDS STEP UP YOUR GAME: LEAD. LOVE. BUILD. FIGHT.

DAY 26

I GAIN THE VICTORY AND KEEP IT

"Not by strength or by might, but by my Spirit," says the LORD of Armies."– Zechariah 4:6 (CSB)

In Nehemiah 4:10 we read about how the *strength* of the laborers was failing. As long as the rubbish was still present, it was draining them of their strength. Until it was gone, they couldn't direct their complete focus or concentrated efforts on building. So it is when we are dealing with *our* rubbish. We, too, may feel like our strength is failing but we must remember a few things. It is not by our own strength and power alone. It is the Lord who strengthens us for battle.

> "It is God who arms me with strength, and makes my way perfect. He makes my feet like the feet of deer, and sets me on high places. He teaches my hands to make war, so that my arms can bend a bow of bronze. You have also given me a shield of Your salvation; Your right hand has held me up, Your gentleness has made me great. You enlarged my path under me, so my feet did not slip." – Psalm 18:32-36 (NKJV)

What a great picture of how God empowers us to gain ground, overcome the enemy, win the victory and keep it.

The road leading to my home at this time is framed by acres of thick brush, trees, and limbs. There are hiking trails that my family enjoys nearby. If you don't stay on the trail, you will encounter tall thickets, briars, and thorns that will tear at your skin. Your feet will likely get tangled in the vines that cover much of the ground and you will trip.

Trust me. It is next to impossible at times to see through the brush, let alone walk through it. I am astounded, though, how most days when I drive down this road deer will scatter, leaping quickly right through the thickest of it. Like a flash, three, four, and even five deer, one after another, take off *running* right through the brush and thickets, disappearing in seconds.

A deer's hooves have a toughness about them that enables them to walk and even run swiftly through the roughest places without danger of tripping or falling. A deer's feet are adapted to moving quickly through rough terrain. The deer can even stand firmly on the rocky places. Unbelievably, their back feet follow exactly where their front feet stepped as they run, creating tremendous stability. All of this gives the deer an advantage in both escaping or combating the enemy. The Word of God says that He will give us these kinds of advantages when we are in the midst of our battles; strategy, stability, safety, and endurance. He will also set us on high places. The Lord of heavenly armies is empowering us by His strength, to gain ground, conquer our enemies, and maintain triumph and rule. God is strong, and He wants us to be strong! He is teaching us to war and to win.

> "God is strong, and he wants you strong. So take everything the Master has set out for you, well-made weapons of the best materials. And put them to use so you will be able to stand up to everything the Devil throws your way. This is no afternoon athletic contest that we'll walk away from and forget about in a couple of hours. This is for keeps, a life-or-death fight to the finish against the Devil and all his angels."

> "Be prepared. You're up against far more than you can handle on your own. Take all the help you can get, every weapon God has issued, so that when it's all over but the shouting you'll still be on your feet. Truth, righteousness, peace, faith, and salvation are more than words. Learn how to apply them. You'll need them throughout your life. God's word is an indispensable weapon. In the same way, prayer is essential in this ongoing warfare. Pray hard and long. Pray for your

brothers and sisters. Keep your eyes open. Keep each other's spirits up so that no one falls behind or drops out." – Ephesians 6:10-12, 13-18 (MSG)

God has given us weapons that are capable of defeating the devil and his devices. They are well-made weapons of the best materials. These weapons are mighty in God for pulling down strongholds (2 Cor. 10:4). The enemy, on the other hand, is counting on our lack of knowledge and our lack of will to use these weapons.

God has, indeed, equipped us well, but it is going to take some personal initiation and action on our part. Are you ready to fight and win the battles that come against you, your marriage, your home and your family? Sometimes that means running swiftly away from evil. Other times that means holding your ground and standing firm. And still, at other times, it involves fighting and even violent combat.

Paul, the writer of the book of Ephesians, often used military terms and metaphors in his letters to the churches. He was very familiar with Roman soldiers and their weapons. He lived in the presence of the greatest military power this world has ever seen. In the latter part of his life, Paul was constantly surrounded by Roman soldiers. On some occasions, he was even chained to his guards. Roman soldiers were very disciplined. They always carried their weapons with them, even in times of peace. Every day they trained and exercised with great diligence, as it if it were the time of war. We need to become as familiar with our weapons and discipline ourselves daily in the Word and prayer.

"God's word is an indispensable weapon. In the same way, prayer is essential in this ongoing warfare" – (Verses 16-17)

The Word of God is alive and active, and sharper than any two-edged sword (Heb. 4:12). It is quick and powerful! It is able to cut down the strongholds of Satan. Don't wait until the heat of the battle to learn how to use your sword. Keep your sword sharpened. Study the Word of God. Memorize it. Pray it. Speak it. Hide it in your heart (Psalm

119:11). Apply it to your life. Strengthen your inner self *before* the enemy attacks.

When Jesus was tempted by Satan in the wilderness, Jesus quoted His Father's words and spoke them with authority. He used the Word of God to counter Satan's attacks. (Matthew 4:4,7, 10)

God's Word is indeed an indispensable weapon. Stand firm in the truth. Protect your heart by walking in the righteousness of God. Prepare yourself with the gospel of peace. Protect your mind with the helmet of salvation. Hold onto that shield of faith. Wield that sword which is the Word of God and pray.

Prayer is absolutely essential in this ongoing warfare. In war, the opposing force likes to knock out the enemy's line of communication. Running interference in this way leaves room for confusion. It gives the opponent a strong advantage to divide and conquer. Don't let the enemy jam up your communication line with the Lord. He is the commander of the Army of God and He knows how to lead us to victory! Prayer accesses what God has already made available to us. If you want victory, make sure you are a man of prayer!

How's your personal prayer life, Man of God? Stay connected to your source of strength and remain submitted to Him.

> "One who submits as a good soldier puts himself in complete subjection to his captain." – Jamieson, Fausset and Brown Commentary

To submit means to yield to one's admonition and control, to be subject to and to obey. We submit our lives to God. We submit our hearts and our will to Him. We submit our struggles and areas of weakness to Him. And by doing so, we can resist the enemy. We can withstand his assaults and push back all hell that rises up against us. We can stand bravely against the enemy. We can push back our adversary. We can fight and win battles. We can walk in victory.

> "Through you we will push back our adversaries." – Psalm 44:5 (NASB)

PRAYER

Lord, I understand that a life submitted to you is a victorious life. When my life is submitted to you, I can move right through the thickest of spiritual warfare unharmed. I can break strongholds and walk in freedom because You have made me free. So today, I completely and totally submit myself to you. I give you my whole life. I am not withholding any part of it from You, Lord. Now gird me with strength. Empower me once again that I might walk in truth, righteousness, peace, and faith. Empower me to win the victory and keep it.

"But the Lord is faithful, and he will strengthen you and protect you from the evil one." – 2 Thess. 3:3 (NASB)

DAY 27

I PROTECT AND DEFEND MY BRIDE

"Keep your heart with all diligence, for out of it springs the issues of life" – Proverbs 4:23 (NKJV)

We submit our lives to Christ and we keep our hearts with all diligence. "With all diligence" means to watch, to guard, and to defend it like a castle. We must keep our own hearts with all diligence and in our role as a husband, we are to watch over and guard our wife's heart as well. We must fight for her heart as we do our own. God has designed us to be the protectors, defenders, and guardians of our wives, our children, and our homes. Are you guarding and protecting your wife's heart?

At times it may be that we need to build a wall of protection around her from people who intend to use, abuse and cause harm to her in some way. John Gill suggests that we are to care for her in a way that would "defend her from all insults and injury." Your wife is perfectly capable of speaking up for herself, defending herself and fighting her own battles. However, when you entered into a covenant with her you made a commitment to defeat each other's enemies. And you, Man of God, have been created to be a natural protector. The Lord will show you when and in what ways you are to do just that; guard, protect, and defend. You are that woman's covering. You must also know when to step in and shield her from the darts of the enemy. A man instinctively knows that he is to physically protect his woman, but does he also understand that he is to protect her spiritually as well? This is an area that many times we overlook. You are a covering for your wife when it comes to the assaults of the enemy. Just as you are to be "watching" and paying attention in your own personal daily life, pay attention to what is happening in your wife's daily life as well. Cover that woman and let the enemy know, "You cannot have my wife. You cannot have my marriage. You cannot have my family. I will fight."

There was a time in scripture when David and his men were away, and the enemy came right into their camp and took their wives and children captive. You can read about it in 1 Samuel chapter 30.

David and his troops were away, preparing themselves to fight yet another battle. Their mission was diverted, though, and they were sent back home. After an exhausting three-day, fifty-mile journey from Aphek to Ziklag, the men arrived, only to find that their city had been destroyed. Smoke was rising from the ashes and worst of all, their wives and children had been taken captive.

> "Now it happened, when David and his men came to Ziklag, on the third day, that the Amalekites had invaded the South and Ziklag, attacked Ziklag and burned it with fire, and had taken captive the women and those who were there, from small to great; they did not kill anyone, but carried them away and went their way. So David and his men came to the city, and there it was, burned with fire; and their wives, their sons, and their daughters had been taken captive. Then David and the people who were with him lifted up their voices and wept, until they had no more power to weep." – 1 Samuel 30:1-4 (NKJV)

It was a terrible scene. The men were so completely wrecked by the loss of their families that they fell to the ground and began to weep and wail until they had no more strength left. Soon this grief turned to rage. The men turned their anger toward David, their leader. They were so overtaken with anger that they talked among themselves of stoning him. David, now dealing with his own grief as well as theirs, turned to God. He prayed, and he inquired of the Lord. He got in God's presence and sought the Lord for direction. David lingered in

God's presence and allowed the Lord to restore his strength. Then the Lord spoke to him about what course of action he should take.

> "So David inquired of the Lord, saying, "Shall I pursue this troop? Shall I overtake them?"
>
> And He answered him, "Pursue, for you shall surely overtake them and without fail recover all." – 1 Samuel 30:8 (NKJV)

David and his troops came upon an Egyptian servant of the Amalekites who had been left behind when he fell sick. This servant was able to lead them straight to the enemy's camp. There were the Amalekites, all spread out, eating, drinking and dancing because of their great spoil. The Word of God tells us that David and his men engaged in battle with the Amalekites from twilight until the evening of the next day, rescuing their wives and children. David brought everything back including great spoils. All was recovered.

Reading through their circumstances, I can't help but wonder about a few things. I wonder what might have happened if David had only remained in his state of grief and never sought the Lord for answers. I wonder what might have happened if the men only continued to blame David and never engaged the real enemy. I wonder what might have happened if they all had just stayed in their place of anger, never moving forward into any kind of action. Eventually, their grief, their sadness, and their anger would have sapped every ounce of their strength. They might have become hardened and bitter, even against God. It is certainly doubtful that they would have recovered anything at all. Instead, they were willing to go right into the enemy's camp and fight. And that is what they did. They went to the enemy's camp and took back what was stolen from them.

Has the enemy managed to come in and steal from you? Is the enemy presently holding your wife captive in any way? What will you do to assure that she is walking in complete freedom?

Aren't you glad that Christ was willing to fight for His bride? Once upon a time, we were captives. We were captive to our sin and subject to the enemy, but Christ came to set the captives free.

"The Spirit of the Lord is upon Me, because the Lord has anointed Me to preach good tidings to the poor; He has sent Me to heal the brokenhearted, to proclaim liberty to the captives, and the opening of the prison to those who are bound; to proclaim the acceptable year of the Lord, and the day of vengeance of our God; to comfort all who mourn." – Isaiah 61:1-2 (NKJV)

Christ laid down His life so that we, His bride, could be free. He did everything necessary to assure that we could be free. Free from guilt. Free from shame. Free from the power of sin. Free from the penalty of sin. Free from the grip of the enemy. Free from the oppressive forces of darkness.

Colossians 2:15 says that "having disarmed principalities and powers, He made a public spectacle out of them, triumphing over them in it." (NKJV)

Christ fought for and rescued His bride! I love what Albert Barnes says about Colossians 2:15: "The Saviour, by his death, wrested the dominion from them, and seized upon what they had captured as a conqueror seizes upon his prey. Satan and his legions had invaded the earth and drawn its inhabitants into captivity, and subjected them to their evil reign. Christ, by his death, subdues the invaders and recaptures those whom they subdued."

Oh, yes! The Lord God is a warrior. He is strong and mighty. And He has won a great victory for us. He not only fights for us, but He fights with us. And like David, we, too, can find our strength in the Lord as we war.

"But David found strength in the Lord his God." – 1 Samuel 30:6 (NIV)

Are we willing to do everything necessary to fight for our bride? Are we willing to fight for her heart? Are we willing to go up against anything that would seek to take her as a captive? Will we guard, protect, and defend her from all evil and every spiritual force of darkness? Will we fight for her? Will we fight for our marriages?

PRAYER

Lord, I will keep my heart with all diligence and I will fight for my wife's heart as I do my own. I am her protector, defender, and guardian. I am her covering. I am willing to do everything necessary to fight for my bride. I will go up against anything that would seek to take her captive. I will guard, protect and defend my wife from all evil and every spiritual force of darkness. I am more than a conqueror and I find my strength in You, Lord God.

DAY 28

I AM MORE THAN A CONQUEROR

"Then the dragon was enraged at the woman and went off to wage war against the rest of her offspring--those who keep God's commands and hold fast their testimony about Jesus."
— Revelation 12:17 (NIV)

The hostility of the devil still exists against God and His church. The dragon in Revelations chapter 12 refers to Satan, and the "woman" is the church or body of believers. We are that offspring and Satan continues to make war with the individual Christian who seeks to keep His commandments and walk in His ways. We are in a war. There is no doubt about it. So, fight the good fight. Conquer and win your own battles and walk in freedom. Defend and protect your bride. Fight for her and fight for your marriage. And remember it is the Lord who gives you the victory.

I love what the Pulpit Commentary has to say about Revelation 12:17. Let these incredible truths encourage you and spur you on, today:

"Our Lord hath overcome him for us, and in his strength we shall overcome too. And we shall be better and stronger Christians for having such a foe to fight. Not only is it the battle that *tries* the soldier, but that *makes* him. We have, however, not just one skirmish, and then peace. Oh no! "Patient continuance in well doing." Daily fighting, daily praying, daily victory, till the end."

We shall be better and stronger because of the battle!

The truth is that Satan could not defeat God and he has never been able to destroy or stop the church. In fact, history has always proved that the more persecution and fiery trials the church experienced, the further it advanced. The stronger it became. In the same way, that can be our story. The story of our lives. The story of our marriages, and what others see when they look at our family. These battles that we fight are for the purpose of making us stronger and better. The only reason the Lord allows us to go through such battles is that He is trying to make us, not break us. If we will press on through, we will find that we have gained something. Every difficulty that my wife and I have walked through has caused our marriage to become stronger and sweeter. Every life struggle that we have fought through has bonded us together even tighter. And our love for one another has increased. This faith walk of endurance and triumph is a legacy that we can pass down. We can't celebrate a victory without first fighting a battle. We cannot call ourselves conquerors without ever having anything to overcome. So, fight the good fight, Men of God.

We are not to be passive. We are to be men of courage. It is time for us to rise up and become the warriors that God has created us to be. That's right. He has hard-wired us to be warriors. It's in us. And it's time for us to act like men.

"Watch ye, stand fast in the faith, quit you like men, be strong." – 1 Corinthians 16:13 (KJV)

This phrase "quit you like men" in 1 Corinthians 16:13 is not referring to the kind of quitting that we might suppose. No. This is the word Adrizomai in the original Greek language and it means to act like a man! It means to play the man, be a man, live like a man, and to be courageous.

"A man is not to be "a coward, or timid, or alarmed at enemies, but [is] to be bold and brave." – Albert Barnes

The idea in 1 Corinthians 16:13 can be summed up in one word; Courage. It is high time that the men of God stand fast in their faith, become stationary and solid in what they believe, and stand firm in their convictions. It is time for the men of God to get a little bit of intestinal fortitude. We must have courage in the midst of pain or adversity. We must exercise bravery, grit, resilience, and endurance. Get some backbone, Men of God! Be strong.

Understand that we have been hard-wired with these very characteristics. It is part of our makeup as men. We have been created by design to be protectors and warriors. We are warriors by nature. We have been created in the image of God, who is both loving and fierce. Christ was the "lion" and the lamb. He is strong and mighty.

"Who is this King of glory? The Lord strong and mighty, the Lord mighty in battle." – Psalm 24:8 (KJV)

"The Lord is a man of war: the Lord is his name." – Exodus 15:3 (KJV)

"The Lord will go forth like a warrior, He will arouse His zeal like a man of war. He will utter a shout, yes, He will raise a war cry. He will prevail against His enemies." – Isaiah 42:13 (NASB)

Prevailed! That is what He did. He completely subdued our enemies by His death. A complete and total victory has been won by Christ. And everything is in subjection to him. By His death and resurrection, He triumphed over all the powers of Hell. Christ has triumphed over all of our foes. He did not leave one enemy unsubdued, therefore we can quit like men; rise up with intestinal fortitude and become fearless in battle.

Jesus said in Matthew 28:18, "All authority has been given to Me". And in Luke 10:19 He said that He has given that power to us.

"Behold, I give you the authority to trample on serpents and scorpions, and over all the power of the enemy, and nothing shall by any means hurt you." – Luke 10:19 (NKJV)

185

The Bible tells us that we can be partakers of His divine nature. He is calling us to walk in His strength, His power, and authority. It's time that we man up and do just that.

"as a man is, so is his strength." – Judges 8:21 (NKJV)

We aren't just talking about physical strength here, guys. It's mental and moral strength. It's strength over temptation. It's strength in the face of tough challenges, pressure, distress, pain, and even fear. It's strength that is found in Christ. We draw that strength and power from Him as we stay connected to Him through His Word and prayer. It has always been said that a man is as strong as his prayer life. So, I will ask you again. How is your prayer life?

God has given us all we need; armor, well-made weapons, insight, discernment, power, and authority. He makes us strong, gives us victory and causes us to triumph. And He calls us "more than conquerors".

"Yet in all these things we are more than conquerors through Him who loved us." – Romans 8:37 (NKJV)

"We are more than conquerors; not only over sin and Satan, but the world, the reproaches, afflictions, and persecutions of it; which they cheerfully and courageously undergo, insomuch that they are not only conquerors, but "more than conquerors": they have above overcome, they have exceedingly the better of it; for they not only patiently bear afflictions and persecutions, but they glory in them; their experience, faith, and joy, are often increased by them; they have sometimes solicited, and even wearied their persecutors; they have got the victory with ease, over Satan and his hellish emissaries, by the blood of the Lamb, and the word of their testimony: but this is not owing to themselves, or through their own strength, but through him that loved us..." – John Gill

We are not "just" conquerors. We are "more than" conquerors. We are abundant gainers. Though we face trials, our faith is not destroyed.

Though we will experience difficulties and even intense warring, we will not be defeated. We are strengthened in all these things. Our love for Christ and for our spouse is increased. We shall have strong, healthy, and thriving marriages. Everything that we put our hands and heart to shall prosper and succeed.

This term "more than conquerors" translates as "vanquished beyond" and "to gain a surpassing victory." Thanks be to God, who gives us the victory through our Lord Jesus Christ. Walk in that victory, men of God. Walk in your role as the husband that God has called you to be. Walk in that strength. Let Christ empower you fresh and anew today. Walk in authority. Walk in the increase and walk in the blessing in Jesus Name.

"Daily fighting, daily praying, daily victory, till the end."

PRAYER

Lord, thank You for the battles in my life, for I am better and stronger because of them. Cause me to become a man of great courage. Help me to always stand fast in my faith. Develop within me every bit of mental and moral strength that I need for my journey. Thank You, Jesus, for subduing the enemy of my soul and gaining such a great victory for me. I will rise up as the warrior that You have created me to be and walk in that victory.

Haven't I commanded you? Strength! Courage! Don't be timid; don't get discouraged. God, your God, is with you every step you take." – Joshua 1:9 (MSG)

DAY 29

I LIVE JOYFULLY WITH MY WIFE

*"Live joyfully with the wife whom you love all the days of your
fleeting life which He has given you under the sun—all the
days of vanity and futility. For this is your reward in life and
in your work in which you have labored under the sun."*
— Ecclesiastes 9:9 (AMP)

Live joyfully with your wife!

The day you were married, most likely your family and friends
gathered together to help you celebrate that special day. Once you
both recited your vows and you kissed your bride, the minister
presented you as Mr. and Mrs. _____. Everyone clapped, cheered,
and celebrated your union and your love for one another. Throughout
the years, the celebrating never ends. You will celebrate many
things together; holidays, anniversaries, the birth of your children,
achievements, a new home, breakthroughs, answered prayers, and it
will continue on and on. Soon, my wife and I will be celebrating the
birth of a new grandchild! Even in the midst of life's difficulties and
challenges, there is always a reason to rejoice.

In John 10:10, Jesus said these words: "The thief comes only to steal
and kill and destroy. I came that they may have life and have it more
abundantly."—He came that we might have life and have it more
abundantly! The abundant life that John 10:10 speaks of is full, rich,
meaningful life, one that's worth living!

The Message Bible says that He came that we would have a "better life than ever dreamed of." Start dreaming again, men of God. And start living with your wife in joy. It is God's purpose that we would have joy in our hearts, that we would have joy in our marriages, and that we would have joy in our homes.

What kind of atmosphere do you create in your home? Is it one of joy?

I read an article recently where women agreed that their husbands caused more stress for them than their children did. According to the article, the most tension that women feel from day to day is when their husbands come home. I asked my wife, "Is this true?" She laughed and began to describe to me what the atmosphere was like in the days when the house was still filled with all the children, and then I would come home from work. It was true. For a time, it wasn't necessarily the kids that were creating the tension. It was me.

I used to have a habit of bringing my work-related aggravation home with me at the end of the day. Apparently, I brought the mood and attitude created in my workplace right through the door with me as I entered my own home. I was instantly creating a negative atmosphere upon arriving and didn't realize it. And the truth is, I am actually a pretty peppy, joyful guy! For a time, though, I was not bringing much joy into my home life. Instead, I was allowing the negative work environment that I had spent my whole day in to affect my home life. I carried it home with me for years. After a time, I began to recognize what I was doing, and I learned to take that stuff off like a coat and hang it up on an imaginary hook on the outside of my front door before I entered. What a change took place. It wasn't my wife or the children after all. It was my grouchy attitude that they were merely responding to. I had a choice to focus on my temporary negative circumstances or focus on the blessings that the Lord had given me. I remember those days and, oh, how I wish that I had enjoyed those days more than I did.

Everyone has a bad day once in a while, but overall, we set a mood in our homes. What type of mood are we setting? If we are feeling miserable, we tend to make everyone around us miserable too. You know it's true. On the other hand, our joy can be contagious. Why don't we begin to come in the door with a smile, a sweet kiss, and tender words, "I'm so glad to see you. I have missed you. You are the most beautiful thing I have seen all day. I couldn't wait to get home!"

The writer of Ecclesiastes encourages us to live joyfully with our wife all the days of our fleeting life. Every year of our lives passes by so quickly. Let's not waste a minute of it focused on the wrong things, forfeiting the abundance Christ made possible for us. The New Living Translation of Ecclesiastes 9:9 uses the words, "Live happily with the woman you love…The wife God gives you is your reward for all your earthly toil."

She is your reward! It's time that we recognize the blessing of marriage itself and become more thankful than ever for the treasure of our own wife. Life is filled with ups and downs, toils and struggles, but your wife is your reward. You are to take delight in her company. You have been through many difficulties, trials and even losses, but guess what? You still have her. And she adds joy and comfort to your life.

Solomon said in Ecclesiastes 4:8, "There is one alone, without companion: He has neither son nor brother. Yet there is no end to all his labors, nor is his eye satisfied with riches. But he never asks, "For whom do I toil and deprive myself of good?" This also is vanity and a grave misfortune." (NKJV)

Solomon continues in verses 9-12, "Two are better than one, because they have a good reward for their labor. For if they fall, one will lift up his companion. But woe to him who is alone when he falls, for he has no one to help him up. Again, if two lie down together, they will keep warm; but how can one be warm alone? Though one may be overpowered by another, two can withstand him. And a threefold cord is not quickly broken."

God loves to give us advantages and what an advantage He has given us through our wives. He expressed from the very beginning that it was not good for man to be alone. So, He gave us an advantage by giving us a helper and a companion. Ecclesiastes reminds us that this beautiful union that we have with our spouse strengthens us in some of the most important ways ever. When you are down, she is there to lift you up. You strengthen each other's hands and hearts. You bear one another's burdens. You comfort one another and restore one another. Together, you are better able to withstand the attacks of the enemy. Whether you realize it or not, your union with your wife helps you to resist temptation. You sharpen one another. Verse 11 speaks of two lying down together and keeping warm together. The physical touch, the warmth of her affection and the pleasure of the intimacy you share with her is powerful, to say the least. Equally as powerful is the idea of this "warmth" becoming a burning fire as a husband and wife spur one another on in their faith:

> "When they are grown cold in their love, lukewarm in their affections, and backward and indifferent to spiritual exercises, yet by Christian conversation may be stirred up to love and good works: so two cold flints struck against each other, fire comes out of them: and even two cold Christians, when they come to talk with each other about spiritual things, and feel one another's spirits, they presently glow in their affections to each other, and to divine things; and especially if Christ joins them with his presence, as he did the two disciples going to Emmaus, then their hearts burn within them." – John Gill

I know this to be true in my own marriage. My wife and I keep passing the fire back and forth as we burn in our relationship with Jesus Christ and our faith remains alive.

Men of God, we are blessed, and we have a reason to rejoice. 1 Thessalonians 5:16 tells us to "rejoice and be glad-hearted continually." Other versions add the words "no matter what." In these scriptures, we find the word *chairō* (rejoice) which translates as "to be full of cheer, to be full of joy, to be glad, and to be calmly happy."

It is God's will that we live joyfully no matter what circumstances we are passing through. Life is full of ups and downs, but our joy can be constant.

Look at Habakkuk 3:17-19:

"Though the fig tree does not blossom and there is no fruit on the vines, though the yield of the olive fails and the fields produce no food, though the flock is cut off from the fold and there are no cattle in the stalls, Yet **I will [choose to] rejoice** in the Lord; **I will [choose to] shout in exultation in the [victorious] God of my salvation!** The Lord God is my strength [my source of courage, my invincible army]; He has made my feet [steady and sure] like hinds' feet and makes me walk [forward with spiritual confidence] on my high places [of challenge and responsibility]." (AMP) emphasis is the author's

It's up to you! It's a choice. It's a decision. Life is too short to let anything stand in the way of your joy. So, from this day forward *decide* to live every day joyfully with your wife.

PRAYER

Lord, I have so much to be thankful for. My wife is a blessing and I choose to celebrate the gift of my marriage every day of my life. I choose to rejoice always and in all circumstances. I am determined to begin living a better life than I ever dreamed of. There is nothing stopping me from living this life of joy. I will live joyfully with my wife. I choose to be full of cheer, to be glad and to be calmly happy! Let the fire burn bright within us and let my wife and I spur one another on in Christ Jesus. Let us truly know this full, rich, meaningful, abundant life and walk in it. And let this joy and abundance spill over and be passed down to our children and grandchildren in Jesus' name.

"Rejoice always, pray without ceasing, give thanks in all circumstances; for this is the will of God in Christ Jesus for you." – 1 Thessalonians 5:16-18 (ESV)

DAY 30

I AM CALLED TO BLESS

*"This day I call the heavens and the earth as witnesses against
you that I have set before you life and death, blessings and curses.
Now choose life, so that you and your children may live."
– Deuteronomy 30:19 (NIV)*

If we have a choice, then the choice is an easy one. We choose life.
We choose to live it joyfully with our wives and we choose to live
under the blessings of the Lord. Not only do we want to live under
the blessings of God, we want to become an instrument of blessing as
well. 1 Peter 3:8-9 tells us that we have been called to bless.

> "Finally, all of you be of one mind, having compassion for one
> another; love as brothers, be tenderhearted, be courteous, not
> returning evil with evil, insult for insult, but on the contrary,
> blessing, knowing that you were called to this, that you might
> inherit a blessing." (NKJV)

Gentlemen, we have been called to bless. Let's talk about that calling.
What exactly does it mean to bless? The word "blessing" here in 1
Peter 3:9 is the original Hebrew word *eulogeo* and it translates as "to
invoke a benediction upon or to speak well of religiously". It is from
the compound of *Eu*, meaning good, and the word *logos*, meaning
something said or something spoken.

This calling that is upon your life and my life is more than just
watching the words that come out our mouths. It's more than just
speaking positively. It's about you and I as born again, spirit-filled
believers learning how to impart a blessing.

There was a time when the impartation of a blessing was practiced often. This kind of spoken blessing is found throughout the Bible. God, Himself, imparted blessings to His people. He verbally blessed Adam and Eve in Genesis 1:28, Noah in Genesis 9:1, Abraham in Genesis 12:1-3, and Jacob in Genesis 32:24-32. In Genesis chapter 14, we find the account of Melchizedek the priest blessing Abraham. Rebecca's family spoke a blessing over her as she prepared to marry Isaac (Genesis 24:60). The people blessed Ruth and Boaz as they were about to marry in the book of Ruth chapter 4. We see fathers and even grandfathers blessing their children and grandchildren in the Bible. Isaac verbally blessed his sons, Jacob and Esau, in Genesis chapter 27. Jacob imparted a spoken blessing over both his son Joseph and his grandchildren in Genesis chapter 48. In the New Testament, we often see Jesus laying hands on children and blessing them. And we see Him speaking a series of blessings over His disciples in Matthew chapter 5. In fact, one of the last things that Jesus did as He ascended to heaven was stretch out His hands and bless His disciples (Luke 24:50-51). Paul opened up his letters to each of the churches by speaking blessings upon them. The blessing was extremely important. Fathers imparted blessings to their children. Priests imparted blessings to their people. Jesus imparted blessings to His disciples, and Paul tells us in 1 Peter 3:8-9 to do the same and not just when it is easy, but even when it is hard.

One of the blessings that we are perhaps most familiar with is found in Numbers 6:22-27:

> "And the Lord spoke to Moses, saying: "Speak to Aaron and his sons, saying, 'This is the way you shall bless the children of Israel. Say to them: "The Lord bless you and keep you; the Lord make His face shine upon you, and be gracious to you; the Lord lift up His countenance upon you, and give you peace." So shall they put My name on the children of Israel and I will bless them." (NKJV)

God commanded Moses and Aaron to speak blessings over the people and this blessing found in Numbers 6:22-27 is often referred to as the high priestly blessing. This blessing was invoked at the end of worship before the people returned to their homes. The people were to carry the blessings with them and every area of their lives would be affected by the words spoken over them. The spoken blessing was felt in their homes, within their families, and in their workplaces. The entire community would be affected by the releasing of the blessing. And this blessing that we see in Numbers 6:24-26 highlighted the importance of the entire family in times of blessing.

Men, today, I want you to know that you are the priest of your home. This rite of the blessing is your heritage and your calling. It is important that you learn how to impart a blessing over your wife and children. The impartation of a spoken blessing is still practiced in the Jewish culture today. Here are some things we should note as we prepare to bless our family:

When fathers would lay hands upon their children and pronounce and speak a blessing over them, they would speak their own wishes for them as well as God's Word. Think about that for a moment. A father only wants the very best for his children. Can you imagine the words that were spoken? There is no doubt that the father saw his child's issues, weaknesses, and personal struggles. These things would be evident to him. The blessing, therefore, would include the speaking of success over every area of struggle and every area of failure. The father was also able to recognize the child's strengths, gifts, potential, and calling, so he would bless the coming forth of those things. Within the blessing, the father would also include the son or daughter's own desires and dreams that they had for their lives.

There is something very powerful about the impartation of a blessing. Do you remember the story of how Isaac's wife Rebecca went to great lengths to come up with a plan to make sure that Isaac spoke the blessing over the youngest son, Jacob? What I find so striking about this particular account is that once spoken, there was something so powerful about the impartation that it was said to be irrevocable once delivered (Genesis 27:33).

Great importance was placed upon the blessing. Children expected God to impart special favor to them as the parents laid hands on them and blessed them. They coveted the spoken blessing. Jacob must have placed great importance upon it because we find him in Genesis chapter 2 wrestling all night long with the angel of the Lord and crying out, "I won't let You go until you bless me." (Genesis 33:26)

Isaac and Jacob blessed their sons. The patriarchs understood the significance of the blessing and spoke over their children, many times going to great lengths to do so. It's time that we learn from the patriarchs and begin to bless not only our children but even our wives.

As Jesus spoke a series of blessings over his disciples in Matthew chapter 5, He spoke over them about their futures. At the time Jesus imparted these blessings over the disciple's lives, they were full of character flaws. Jesus was able to look past all of their shortcomings, however, and see the real potential that existed within them. He blessed them and said things like, "You are the salt of the earth and you are the light of the world" (verses 13-14). At the time He spoke these words, His disciples were neither of these things, but He was declaring that they would become effective witnesses in the world. In spite of their current faults and failures, He was able to see the great possibilities that were ahead for those men. He blessed them and eventually they became everything that He spoke over them.

As parents, we must ask God to give us the ability to see the successful future of our children. Let's inquire of the Lord what His plan and purposes are for their lives and begin to speak a blessing over them. Husbands, impart a blessing to your wives. Lay hands on her and pray for her. Speak the Word of God over her. Impart a spoken blessing over her and do it often.

My wife and I have been doing this for several years now. Not only do we prepare blessings to speak over our children, but we prepare blessings that we speak over one another. I have to tell you that in an unexpected way it has created an even stronger bond between us. There is something very intimate about imparting spoken blessings over your spouse. There is a greater oneness that is experienced. There is an intense love that is felt as the blessing is imparted. This practice is more than just a good idea, it is my calling and it is your calling.

I want to encourage you to sit down and write out a blessing to speak over your spouse. Give it some prayer and some thought. Seek the Lord and ask Him what His desire is for her. Be Spirit-led. Include what is in your heart for her and what you desire to see released in her life. Also, ask her what she has is in her heart, what she is desiring and what her dreams might be. Then you can begin to bless the success and fruitfulness of those very things. Ask her about the areas in which she is really struggling. Speak success over those areas. Consider what her strengths, giftings, potential, and calling might be. Bless the coming forth of those things. Once you have prepared a blessing, lay hands on her and impart the blessing. As you speak over her, God will activate the blessing. Make this practice of blessing a habit and watch what the Lord will do. And remember that in some way, your own blessing is tied to blessing others.

> "Finally, all of you be of one mind, having compassion for one another; love as brothers, be tenderhearted, be courteous, not returning evil with evil, insult for insult, but on the contrary, blessing, knowing that you were called to this, **that you might inherit a blessing.**"

PRAYER

Lord, continue to speak to me about this practice of blessing my wife and family. I choose life today; abundant life, full, meaningful life and a blessed life. I desire to be a blessing to my wife and my family. Begin to show me what You have in mind for my wife, Lord. Show me what Your heart is toward her. Reveal her struggles and weak areas to me that I might begin to bless those areas in a way that leads to strength and success. Help me to know the dreams and desires that she has in her heart that I might bless the coming forth of those things. Cause me to see her gifts and speak life and fruitfulness over every area. Let me use the power of my words to bless rather than curse. Be present to activate Your blessings in our marriage and our lives as we follow You, obey Your commandments, and walk in the very things that You have created us for. Protect us from evil and make Your face shine upon us. Extend Your favor to us, Lord. Be gracious to us, give us peace, and be with us where ever we go.

CHAPTER 31

I AM A FAITHFUL MAN

"Most men will proclaim each his own goodness, but who can find a faithful man?" – Proverbs 20:6 (NKJV)

A lot of men talk a good talk, but talk is cheap. Actions speak louder. True character is seen. A faithful man, as defined in Proverbs 20:6 is a man who is steadfast. He keeps his promises and fulfills his obligations. He is a man of truth and he is truly reliable. He is loyal and loving. He shows kindness and is merciful. A faithful man has a good reputation and leaves behind a good name.

This word "faithful" in the original Hebrew language is the word *'êmûn* and it translates as faithful and trusty. It is from the root word *'aman* meaning "to build up or support; to foster as a parent or nurse; figuratively to render (or be) firm or faithful, to trust or believe, to be permanent or quiet; morally to be true or certain; be faithful, (of long continuance, steadfast, sure, trusty, verified), nurse (-ing father) established."

These are the same characteristics that we have seen outlined again and again throughout this study. In our role as husbands, we are to be faithful men!

According to Proverbs 20:6, the faithful man is not a man who merely toots his own horn creating an outward appearance that he is really *something*. This scripture seems to imply that most men do just that. They like to project an image of themselves that doesn't necessarily line up with their true character.

I used to work for a car manufacturer that made some very bold claims about their vehicles. That company stated that when you drove their car you were "driving the ultimate driving machine". The success of that company was poised on their ability to back up those claims. They did, indeed, build a car that was top notch and well worth the cost. From working on the inside of this car manufacturing plant for five years, I can testify that their claims are accurate. Each car that left that facility wasn't just a good-looking car on the outside, but they were quality-built vehicles. When you looked at the company's profit and loss statement you could quickly ascertain one thing. Profits were astronomical. They were who they said they were and it showed in the bottom line. When it comes to your role as a husband, it doesn't really matter what you might claim to be true about yourself. Does your character back up those claims? Is the man that others see from the outside line up with what your wife is seeing from the inside, behind closed doors? It is a man's character that speaks and testifies of his goodness. Proverbs 20:6 gives us the impression that a man of character is a rare find. This is certainly true, today. I think that you would agree that our world needs more faithful men.

My challenge to you today, gentlemen, is to become part of that rare breed of faithful men and let everything you do be done in excellence. In a time of moral decay in our nation, let's rise up and be the men that God is calling us to be. Let's be faithful leaders, faithful builders, faithful lovers, and faithful warriors.

Husbands, be faithful in providing leadership in your home and marriage. God, Himself, has appointed you to this significant role. It is a God-given role filled with divine purpose. Be responsible. Be the kind of man that your wife can trust. Be a man of integrity and honesty, and a man who is worthy of respect. Rule your own home well. Be a man who is committed to your spouse, attentive to your children and diligent in looking after your own affairs. Your ministry begins in and flows out of your home. Start there. Seek first the kingdom of God and His righteousness. Make the Lord your main pursuit. Be faithful in your relationship with Him and remember that the fear of the Lord is the beginning of wisdom. Wisdom, knowledge, and understanding come from the Lord. Lead with His wisdom and knowledge. Lead your wife as the Lord leads you. Seize your opportunity and privilege to lead her, not in a domineering fashion but as a faithful servant-leader. Be humble. Lead with a shepherd's heart. Be mindful that you have been put in charge of a soul more precious to you than any other. Be the spiritual leader in your home. Have a vision for your future and lead with purpose.

Be a faithful lover. Love your wife as Christ loved the church. His love is a deep, enduring, and sacrificial love. Love her like that. Love your wife God's way. Let it be an extravagant love. Love her with a generous love and don't hold back. Be willing to make any and every sacrifice necessary for her. Seek her highest good. Surround her with a caring, unselfish love. Be willing to demonstrate your total devotion to your bride. Be a forgiving and compassionate spouse. Release your wife from all of the blame, imperfections, and failures she is guilty of and allow God to bring new life into your relationship every day. Nourish and cherish your wife. Take care of her physical needs and also nourish her spiritually, mentally, and emotionally. Cleave to her and yoke yourself together with her, truly becoming one. Guard the unity of your marriage at all costs. Protect the sanctity of your marriage. Keep your covenant of love, honoring your wedding vows all the days of your life. Follow through with every promise. And remember, your love story is but a reflection of the greatest love story ever told. You are an image bearer.

Be a faithful builder. Build your marriage on the sure foundation of Jesus Christ. Take care in the way that you build. Build it well and build it right. Follow the blueprint that Christ has given you in His Word. Be faithful in all of the small things and watch it all come together. Honor God, honor your marriage and honor your wife. Treat your spouse with behavior worthy of respect and esteem. Walk in an attitude of lovingkindness toward her. Demonstrate honor and respect through your actions and your words. Recognize that your words have the power to build up or tear down, wound or heal, burden or refresh. Do not be harsh with your wife. Minister to her heart with your words. Become a good communicator. Keep working on it! Learn to share your heart and be a ready listener. Enjoy your wife's company. Be intentional with the time and attention you give to her. Make her your top priority. All these things foster intimacy. Be sure to handle conflict correctly, readily admit your faults, and take responsibility for your wrongs. Be quick to repent and make things right. Ask for forgiveness. Don't give the enemy a foothold. Be faithful to extend grace and forgiveness as well. Deal with your issues and keep your heart pure before the Lord. Become a man after God's own heart. Be consistent in the reading of the Word, establish family worship, and be a man of prayer. Pray with your wife. You initiate it. Make your home a place where the Holy Spirit is welcome and dwells. Be filled with His Spirit and walk in His power. Be steadfast in these things. Dedicate your marriage and all that you are building to the Lord and build well.

Be a faithful warrior. Watch and pray. Be prepared for battle. Take your position and exercise your authority. Be strong. Walk in the Lord's power and might and fight the good fight of faith. Stand firm in the truth. Do not let the enemy come in and take territory. Stand guard, resist, and push back the enemy in your life and marriage. Conquer and win your own personal battles. Rule over sin in your own life. Gain the victory and keep it. Press forward. Keep your heart with all diligence. Honor God with your body. Guard the sexual intimacy in your marriage relationship. Be faithful, true and loyal to your wife. Fight for her heart. Guard, protect and defend her from evil and every force of spiritual darkness. Fight for your bride and fight for your marriage. Become a man of great courage. Submit all areas of your life to God and develop mental and moral strength. Live a disciplined life. Live with your wife in joy! Bless that woman and store up a godly inheritance for your children, grandchildren, and generations to come. Be a faithful man.

Proverbs 3:3-4 says, "Let love and faithfulness never leave you; bind them around your neck, write them on the tablet of your heart. Then you will win favor and a good name in the sight of God and man."

You've got this, Man of God. You've been called, appointed and anointed for this role, so walk in it. Step up your game! Lead, love, build and fight.

PRAYER

Here I am Lord. I will lead, love, build and fight in Jesus' Name. I will be a faithful man; faithful in the things that You are calling me to. I will be faithful in my role as a husband and I will be faithful to honor You in it. Thank you, Lord, for giving me the tools I need to have the marriage that You have purposed for me to have. Continue to extend Your blessing and favor to me that I might enjoy a strong, loving, healthy marriage that thrives and that I might truly become Your image bearer upon the earth. In Jesus' Name, I pray.

HUSBANDS STEP UP YOUR GAME: LEAD. LOVE. BUILD. FIGHT.

NOTES

Introduction: Let's Just Go Ahead and Be What We Were Made to Be

    1. Emasculate; https://en.oxforddictionaries.com/definition/emasculate

Day 1: I am Called to Lead

    1. Leader; https://www.vocabulary.com/dictionary/leader

Day 2: I am a Man with a Vision

    1. Leader; https://www.merriam-webster.com/dictionary/leader

Day 3: I am a Man of Integrity

    1. Integrity; https://en.oxforddictionaries.com/definition/integrity
    2. Brown-Driver-Briggs' Hebrew Definitions, H8537; Integrity
    3. Strong's Hebrew and Greek Dictionaries, G4291; Rule
    4. Thayer's Greek Definitions, G4291; Rule
    5. Strong's Hebrew and Greek Dictionaries, G2212; Seek
    6. Thayer's Greek Definitions, G2212; Seek
    7. Sermon Bible Commentary, Matthew 6:33; Seek

Day 5: I Lead with Wisdom and Knowledge

    1. http://www.pewresearch.org
    2. http://www.whale.to/b/importance_of_fathers.html
    3. https://www.romancatholicman.com/dad-takes-faith-god-seriously-will-children/

Day 6: I Lead with a Purpose

    1. Expositor's Bible Commentary, Ephesians 5

Day 7: I Lead with Purpose

    1. Strong's Hebrew and Greek Dictionaries, G2776; Head
    2. Strong's Hebrew and Greek Dictionaries, H2896; Good
    3. Brown-Driver-Briggs' Hebrew Definitions, H2896; Good
    4. Strong's Hebrew and Greek Dictionaries, H7522; Favor
    5. Brown-Driver-Briggs' Hebrew Definitions, H7522; Favor
    6. Matthew Henry's Commentary on the Whole Bible, Proverbs 18:22

7. John Wesley's Explanatory Notes, Proverbs 18:22
8. Matthew Henry's Commentary on the Whole Bible, Ephesians 5:22,23

Day 8: I Imitate Christ as I Love My Bride

1. Strong's Hebrew and Greek Dictionaries, G3402; Imitator

Day 9: I am a Forgiving and Compassionate Spouse

1. Strong's Hebrew and Greek Dictionaries, G26; Love
2. Albert Barnes' Notes on the Bible, Ephesians 5:26
3. Samuele Bacchiocchi, *The Marriage Covenant*, Biblical Perspectives, 1991
4. Matthew Henry's Commentary on the Whole Bible, Ephesians 5:25

Day 10: I Nourish and Cherish My Wife

1. Expositor's Bible Commentary, Ephesians 5:25-26
2. Strong's Hebrew and Greek Dictionaries, G1625, G1537, G5142; Nourish
3. Thayer's Greek Definitions, G2282; Cherish
4. Cherish; https://en.oxforddictionaries.com/definition/cherish
5. Albert Barnes' Notes on the Bible, Ephesians 5:23

Day 11: My Wife is My Priority

1. Strong's Hebrew and Greek Dictionary, G4347; Joined
2. Strong's Hebrew and Greek Dictionary, G4801; Yoke together
3. Strong's Hebrew and Greek Dictionary, H1692; Cleave
4. Kingdom Dynamics, Male and Female, "God's Image Bearers in the Earth", Jack Hayford, New Spirit Filled Life Bible, page 5, Thomas Nelson, Inc., 2002

Day 13: I am a Covenant Keeper

1. Samuel Bacchiochi, *The Marriage Covenant*, Biblical Perspectives, 1991, Chapters 1 and 2
2. https://www.biblicalperspectives.com/books/marriage/1.html
3. Brant Pitre, *Jesus the Bridegroom*, Crown Publishing, 2014

Day 14: I Will Not Be Driven Off Course

1. Matthew Henry's Commentary on the Whole Bible; 1 Corinthians 13:4
2. John Wesley's Explanatory Notes; 1 Corinthians 13:4
3. Albert Barnes' Notes on the Bible; 1 Corinthians 13:4
4. Thayer's Greek Definitions, G3114; Suffereth long
5. Strong's Hebrew and Greek Dictionary, G3516; Child

6. Strong's Hebrew and Greek Dictionary, G4722; Beareth
7. Strong's Hebrew and Greek Dictionary, G5278; Endureth
8. Strong's Hebrew and Greek Dictionary, G1601; Fails

Day 15: I Build My Marriage on a Sure Foundation

1. "My Hope is Build on Nothing Less", Edward Mote, 1834

Day 16: I am a Wise Builder

1. Jamieson, Faussett, and Brown Commentary, Colossians 3:19

Day 18: I Handle Conflict Correctly

1. Strong's Hebrew and Greek Dictionary, H4832; Health

Day 19: I am a Man Who Walks in Forgiveness

1. Thayer's Greek Definitions, G5483; Forgive
2. Kingdom Dynamics, "Forgiveness", Raleigh B. Washington, New Spirit Filled Life Bible, page 1675, Thomas Nelson Inc., 2002

Day 20: I Guard the Unity in My Marriage

1. John Gill's Exposition of the Entire Bible, Mark 3:25
2. Albert Barnes' Notes on the Bible, 1 Peter 3:7

Day 21: I Dedicate all that I am Building to the Lord

1. Albert Barnes' Notes on the Bible, 1 Peter 3:7

Day 24: I am Winning My Own Personal Battles

1. The Pulpit Commentary, Matthew 11:12
2. Adam Clarke's Commentary on the Bible, Matthew 11:12
3. C.J. Vaughan, Cambridge Review, May 5, 1886, Matthew 11:12

Day 25: I Keep Myself Pure

1. Family Research Council, "The Effects of Pornography on Individuals, Marriage, Family and Community", March 2011, Patrick F. Fagan, Ph.D., www.frc.org, 803-225-4008, 801 G Street, NW, Washington, D.C. 20001
2. Strong's Hebrew and Greek Dictionary, G283; Pure

Day 26: I Gain the Victory and I Keep It

1. Jamieson, Fausset and Brown Commentary, James 4:7
2. Thayer's Greek Definitions, G5293; Submit

Day 27: I Protect and Defend My Bride

1. John Gill's Exposition of the Entire Bible, 1 Corinthians 11:3
2. Albert Barnes' Notes on the Bible, Colossians 2:15

Day 28: I am More than a Conqueror

1. The Pulpit Commentary, Revelation 12:17
2. Strong's Hebrew and Greek Dictionaries, G407; Quit you like men
3. Thayer's Greek Definitions, G407; Quit you like men
4. Albert Barnes' Notes on the Bible, 1 Corinthians 16:13
5. John Gill's Exposition of the Entire Bible, Romans 8:37
6. Strong's Hebrew and Greek Dictionaries, G5245; More than conquerors
7. Thayer's Greek Definitions, G5245; More than conquerors

Day 29: I Live Joyfully with My Wife

1. John Gill's Exposition of the Entire Bible, Ecclesiastes 4:11
2. Strong's Hebrew and Greek Dictionaries, G5463; Rejoice

Day 30: I am Called to Bless

1. Strong's Hebrew and Greek Dictionaries, G2127; Blessing

Day 31: I am a Faithful Man

1. Strong's Hebrew and Greek Dictionaries, H529 and H539; Faithful

ABOUT THE AUTHORS

Gary and Jennifer Rash are pastors serving the upstate of South Carolina for the last 29 years. Currently, they serve as Revival Hub Directors for God Invasion Revival Center, a place where pastors, leaders, and people come together for renewing, refreshing, rekindling, re-igniting, reviving, and receive fresh fire. Gary and Jennifer have a heart to see a true spiritual awakening sweep across our nation and land. Gary also has a heart for men's ministry, marriage ministry, and the family. He has been involved in church planting, pastoring and mentoring young men. He and his wife Jennifer have been married for 30 years, have three sons, and reside in the Spartanburg, SC, area. Jennifer speaks at women's conferences, leads Bible studies, women's groups and mentors young women. She is also the author of a best-selling book, *The Path to Becoming a Proverbs 31 Wife*. Today, Gary and Jennifer travel, preaching and teaching the Word of God and can be contacted at garyrashministries@gmail.com as well as jenniferrashministries@gmail.com.

Made in the USA
San Bernardino, CA
24 October 2018